Good News from the Barrio

GOOD NEWS FROM THE BARRIO

Prophetic Witness for the Church

Harold J. Recinos

WESTMINSTER
JOHN KNOX PRESS
LOUISVILLE • KENTUCKY

© 2006 Harold J. Recinos

Book design by Sharon Adams
Cover design by designpointinc.com
Cover art courtesy of Los Trabadores

First edition
Published by Westminster John Knox Press
Louisville, Kentucky

This book is printed on acid-free paper that meets the American National Standards Institute Z39.48 standard. ♾

PRINTED IN THE UNITED STATES OF AMERICA

06 07 08 09 10 11 12 13 14 15—10 9 8 7 6 5 4 3 2 1

Library of Congress Cataloging-in-Publication Data

Recinos, Harold J. (Harold Joseph).
    Good news from the barrio : prophetic witness for the church / Harold J. Recinos.— 1st ed.
        p. cm.
    Includes bibliographical references and index.
    ISBN–13: 978-0-664-22940-5 (alk. paper)
    ISBN–10: 0-664-22940-9
    1. Church work with Hispanic Americans. I. Title.

BV4468.2.H57R42 2006
277.3'083'08968—dc22
                                                    2005042309

For
Elijah Joshua Recinos

Contents

CROWDED BEDS

I cannot forget cold winter
nights in the fifth-floor
apartment where roaches often

fell from the ceiling on
our crowded beds. mami, who
was hardly able to greet

the day in our eyes, rode
the subway downtown each
day to earn just enough

money to yell nightly at
life beneath the sheets covering
her lover. firm in her faith

of better days to come she
held parties with beer, rum,
music, food, and friends not

named in English. she kept
an altar in the bedroom where
we all slept mixed with saints

and a sacred heart Jesus to
pray for a cure to family storms.
once we found Kennedy half-dollar

coins hidden beneath a hollow
stand of one saint who was to
bring good luck to the poor.

we went to school in this
place called the South Bronx
ready to speak the Spanish words

in our heads to teachers we
soon detected deaf to sounds not
made in English. every day

they chattered about American
history in black and white leaving us
in wonder over being disappeared from

the face of the states. yet we
grew with salsa music and learned
to see and speak in canons of thought

denied us. then one unforeseen
day a heroin plague with many
names attacked all the kids'

veins in the neighborhood as
mothers wept in official places
where educated blancos said

little to them. downtown the
presses reported the growing
drug trade by counting stiffs

found on garbage heaps left
on the streets by people weary
of living in the long day of

the dead. in the crowded beds
at night people whispered so
God would not hear words that

said the plague was more powerful
than the church that no longer gave
us life despite all the candles

lighted. the night before
burials we cried looking out
the window at the neon sign

of the Ortiz Funeral Home where
Rosa, Joseph, Lefty, Rudy, Julia,
Manolo, Jimmy, Shorty, and all

dead friends ended. they departed
all dressed up like the white
downtown crowd for the trip to

the graveyard where you don't
tell time and visitors walk
pondering the loyalty of God.

emerging from the apartments
where rats know how to come
and go we stop on the corner

to coldly think about undoing
the stiff penalty pronounced
against our generation.

Introduction

1

In the United States it does not take much effort to know little about Latinos. Because Latino lives are so meshed socially, politically, economically, and theologically with that of other members of U.S. society, the cultural and historical illiteracy about the Latino community seems even more remarkable. Non-Latinos in the United States rely heavily on stereotypes and fear to shape the knowledge they have about us. Latinos are viewed by too many of their neighbors as the disruptive outsiders who take jobs away from Americans, bringers of Latin America's social problems to U.S. soil, or simply strangers unwilling to adapt to U.S. society.

As a Puerto Rican, I grew up thinking of myself as a person unworthy of American society. I attended public schools in the South Bronx where the image of "America" was forged in white Protestant Anglo-Saxon terms and Latinos were treated in the curriculum as "foreign others." Although Latinos first explored and settled what was later to become the United States, the standard educational practice taught one to think of Latinos as recent arrivals. We discussed on the South Bronx stoops the idea that Latinos made their influence known more than five hundred years ago in the North American territory, yet textbooks made no mention of these historical figures who contributed to the formation of American national identity. Our questions had to be answered on the street corners by old men playing dominos or grandmothers staring down from their windows.

In the twenty-first century, the people of the barrio add their voice to discussions about the meaning of national identity and tell more established members of society not to imagine community in ways that render Latinos invisible. In our land of different languages, customs, religions, and peoples, building the future in American society means accepting nothing better than our diversity. Most of us live and work today in a multiracial America, but the public discourse defining America's politics of race mostly reflects the concerns of black and white Americans. When we remove the scales from our eyes, the view that America is a white society or that race matters only in black and white will find little ground to stand on. America was not built by white persons alone, and different communities of color shaped national identity and nourished the political struggle that made democratic and religious institutions possible.

I remember conversations in the South Bronx in which we questioned the white representation of Americanness being fed to us, beginning with stories about the Pilgrims. We also joked about growing up invisible in America, because if you are not black or white you are not seen. If there are any conversations taking place of this kind on South Bronx stoops today, they likely turn to the stereotypical terms produced by the American racial hierarchy that says whites are true Americans, African Americans are inferior Americans, Asians are recent arrivals, Latinos are a suspect class, and Native Americans are out of mind. Today such conversations could affirm that national identity was conceived in the contradiction between the idea of equal and inalienable rights for all people, while Native Americans were being exterminated, blacks enslaved, Latinos disinherited, and Asians exploited and killed.

American society needs desperately to come to terms with its plural self, especially given that by the year 2050 white Americans will be a minority and people of color will be in the majority.[1] The demographic changes that are beginning to be felt in American society are already filling some members of society with a fear that ethnic pluralism spells trouble. The 1990s saw a backlash especially against nonwhite immigrants that reflected the idea voiced by conservative think tanks and not a few church corridors that America has simply gone too far in welcoming or accepting nonwhite groups to its shores. Peter Brimelow's book *Alien Nation* flatly argues that immigrants of color, especially Hispanics, are destroying America.

The backlash in recent history unfolded in the form of a new racist nationalism driven by four cultural beliefs: first, the strong feeling among many Americans of European descent that certain "peoples" from Latin America, Asia, and Africa are racially and culturally inferior; second, the belief that these "inferior races" are simply unable to assimilate to the dominant white culture; third, the perception that members of these "inferior races" are responsible for taking jobs away from native-born Americans and that they cause national economic decline; lastly, the belief that these undesirable groups stress the welfare and school systems and may someday politically threaten the dominant culture.[2] This nativist cultural climate has given rise to increased racial violence and discrimination against people of racial and ethnic minorities and mounting feelings of resentment and alienation among communities of color.

Today some U.S. citizens who fear crossing racial and ethnic boundaries think power is being taken away from deserving whites and given to undeserving people of color. They believe people of color threaten American culture or represent a foreign invasion; thus, the state needs to operate on the principle of exclusion of other cultures, languages, and people. In American public schools, for instance, the battles lines are routinely drawn around the question of multicultural education. Although multicultural education represents an attempt to deal with a diversity of voices in order to better understand American culture, its attackers warn that it will ultimately foster the collapse of American institutions and society. For this group of citizens, public education should focus on white particularity and definitions of national identity over against the particularity and varied historical experiences of the many other population groups who built up the country.

In America today we are all faced with the choice between creating life together on the basis of hate for other cultures, languages, and ethnic groups, or working hard to become a free union out of many. It is here that I think the message of the church needs to address the current national climate of increasing racial polarization by challenging people to choose between standing with those social groups who wish to shatter dreams, or walking with others who long to build society on the beauty of its diversity. The church is called to evangelize American culture by proclaiming the good news that plainly reveals that what will make our differences possible in the United States is a politics of crossing cultural and racial borders in the interest of securing a more inclusive community.

Although Latinos are reduced to insignificance by scholars of the dominant culture in the church, their view on the evangelization of culture has cultural relevance for mainline Christianity facing a crisis-ridden future. Latino evangelization centers attention on the work of God, who aims to repair broken relationships and disunity in a diversely created world. If post-Enlightenment culture is characteristically doubtful about the person and mission of Jesus Christ, Latinos are indignant with the witness of mainline Christians who do not call up the good news of Jesus Christ in the multicultural context and the Latino world of poverty, violence, and struggle for liberation. Barrio evangelization says that Christ is present and accessible to the mainline church in the poor of the barrio who are sinned against, marginalized, and oppressed (see Matt. 25:31–46).

As many theologians of the dominant culture have taken us down the road of uncertainty and ambiguity, Latinos beg them to open the eyes of academic reason to the world of the crucified poor. On the occasions when the people of the barrio are driven away like useless strangers from the mainline church, Latinos remind more than a few church leaders that such behavior nailed Christ to the cross. Barrio Christians say that financial stability is not what enables people beyond the walls of mainline churches to see God in history; instead, when mainline Christians open their eyes to the miserable reality of the racially despised and poor God becomes *Emmanuel* and the church acts to offer justice and love to human beings. Keep in mind that the world of wealth that shapes glad memories in affluent churches and religious organizations is less familiar to Jesus Christ than the situation of the poor, sick, sad, and outcast.

In the barrio where people live on the edge of death and their humanity is not of compelling interest to mainline churches, evangelization means deepening and intensifying the commitment to the reign of God by way of a preferential option of love for the excluded. Mainline Christians concerned to work in the direction of the new life promised by the gospel can look to the barrio today for new understanding. People in the barrio know and address a God of life who is not like the God proclaimed in many dominant culture churches, who is imaged as an adversary of racial equality and a defender of economic injustice. For the people of the barrio, evangelization means proclaiming the kingdom of God in a world divided by race, class, and gender. Thus, God's reign is understood as the antithesis of all that denies life and promotes separating walls of hostility.

Barrio Christians believe that local congregations need to engage in a public ministry in which church leadership claims a public voice and engages in social action beyond conventional religious settings. Of course, in the late nineteenth and early twentieth centuries, mainline Protestant denominations engaged in various forms of social activism that contributed important collective values and public theological voices to the wider American society. In this period, mainline Protestant denominations experienced an easy crossing of the bridge between religion and culture; however, the bridge led from dominant cultural identity to the moral camps of established society. Today barrio Christianity calls for the renewal of the church and culture from a point of departure in the miserable reality of forgotten people.

Since the 1960s, mainline churches have struggled to understand the ways they have legitimated the dominant culture's history of oppressive practices against black, Asian, and Native American humanity. In the 1980s, Central American refugees who claimed that American Christians' theological views mostly justified the governmental policies that fueled unjust civil wars in the Central American region confronted mainline churches. More recently, they have faced the world unable to find a common voice for naming evil and speechless before religious violence in the world. Today the people in the barrio say that in ways not previously thought theological leadership will need to consider far more seriously the contributions of what the anthropologist Eric Wolf named "the people without history," the people on whom the economy depends and the mainline church renders voiceless and invisible.

The reality of the barrio reminds mainline churches that Christ died at the margins of established society to give all people life—especially the neglected, powerless, and poor. Because social interaction takes place in a context of racial and ethnic differences in the United States and world, barrio evangelization suggests that public faith witness should help to increase critical reflection on plural public practices and cultural meaning in light of the gospel imperatives of justice and love. Hence, as mainline churches prepare for a different future, the barrio cries out for the congregations to make space for diverse cultural voices to speak and be heard, voices that critique established ideologies, voices that promote a hermeneutics of justice and diversity; voices that opt for a church that struggles for a more just future in a less violent world.

Whatever its denominational expression, barrio evangelization includes recognition of a relationship with God that grows out of the unique historical experience and social reality of the Latino struggle for justice and dignity. I invite the reader to cross the ethnic boundary to walk with Latinos in the barrio and through this experience to surrender to the demands of the gospel. The unexpected news of Christ that is now hidden in the Latino slums will plainly reveal God among downtrodden and outcast people. The barrio poor are good news from God for mainline churches in need of being pulled away from the seduction of wealth, power, and prestige to the authentic ground of the cross. The prophetic imagination of mainline churches is discoverable by openness and commitment to the barrio.

Chapter 1 explores the issue of evangelization from the perspective of the barrio by first examining the politics of race in the United States. Both Alexis de Tocqueville and Gunnar Myrdal concluded that the successes of American democratic and Christian cultures never wiped out racist behavior. Because racism is a contemporary problem in society and the church, I will show that we are not now living in a postracial world. In exploring the themes and history relative to America's politics of race, I will seek both to expose the evils of racism and to challenge the established biracial framing of the politics of race relations in society. Race matters in more than black and white, evidenced by the racial lines dividing neighborhoods, schools, churches, entertainment, ethnicity, and culture in America. My discussion of aspects of the historical sociology of race seeks to contextualize the barrio and its offer of fresh biblical interpretations and vision for a prophetic evangelizing stance on social justice issues.

Chapter 2 discusses evangelization as "prophetic imagination" by focusing on the centrality of the Latino poor in theological identity and in light of the idea of proclaiming the reign of God. One of the central themes to be explored in this chapter is speaking of God in the midst of unjust suffering and the ongoing experience of crucifixion that typifies life at the margins of an affluent society. The meaning of barrio evangelization that issues forth from this context suggests God loves the poor in a special way and calls the church to accompany the people in the barrio in the interest of becoming good news for them. In Chapter 3, my discussion of evangelization will explore the political dimension of the gospel, which promotes solidarity with the poor who expose the truth about structures of sin and who use their political imagination to envision a new future society. My discussion of barrio evangelism departs from the situation of power and powerlessness, hope and despair, poverty and insecurity that characterizes the Latino margin of American society.

Chapter 4 will explore evangelization in light of barrio spirituality, drawing attention to the lived experience of Latino newcomers taking up residence in American society. These are the people whose experience resonates with the words of Paul, "We are treated as imposters, and yet are true; as unknown, and yet are well known; as dying, and see—we are alive; as punished, and yet not killed" (2 Cor. 6:8–9). Finally, chapter 5 outlines how mainline Christians are faced with the challenge of embracing cultural pluralism. It outlines a cultural anthropological approach for the study of human diversity and for understanding evangelization in light of God's reconciling work. Because the Great Commission is not a mandate to eradicate other cultures, local congregations need to understand cultural differences to effectively share the message of God's love for human beings.

In the post–September 11 world, some individuals have returned to churches, and many more feel religion has lost its credibility. This is quite understandable given that in the name of God followers of various religious traditions have been associated in Central Asia, Eastern Europe, the Middle East, Africa, and the United States with inhumanity, repression, and death. Recently, the Roman Catholic Church's sex scandals and Billy Graham's taped comments about "Satanic Jews" controlling the media have further eroded the moral authority and confidence of Americans in the leadership of established and revivalist faith traditions. I hope this book will inspire readers to work for God's reign of justice and reconciliation, while also searching the dark corners of their souls for the compassion needed to live in difficult times.

CLEAN

on the corner
there is a spot
on the sidewalk

without trash
no one ever
steps on not

even the wind
blows broken glass
to it. this corner

with twenty-twenty
vision is the place
we think of the dead

that weigh more
than all the
churches in the

city where people
shut their eyes
and seldom come

out alive.

1

Walk with Christ from the Color Line to the Borderline

In his book *Christianity in the Twenty-first Century* (1993), sociologist Robert Wuthnow suggests that American Christianity is facing a future filled with challenges that require rethinking where to engage in mission. Although these challenges are too numerous to mention, the most obvious ones are the global AIDS epidemic, environmental destruction, and weapons of mass destruction. I would add to the list fundamentalist extremism, religious and ethnic violence, and global terrorism. American Christianity is challenged to elevate these dimensions of social and cultural reality to the level of theological thought by strategizing ways to promote critical insights into the meaning of Christian mission and community in a diverse and conflicted world.[1] Latino Christians can be helpful in providing critical insights into the future of Christianity in American society.

Mainline churches facing worldly trials must clarify how they follow Jesus Christ and talk about the saving acts of God. As a Latino theologian, my focus in theological reflection is on the historical experience of the crucified people in the barrio. In academic and church circles, I have argued that church leadership for the sake of the world requires taking seriously the contributions of what anthropologist Eric Wolf has named "the people without history," the people on whom the economy depends and mainline churches ignore. As many culturally established theologians have taken the leadership of the contemporary church down a placid road, I have suggested to those willing to listen that Jesus begs us to open our eyes to the world of strangers and outcasts. I believe Christianity in the third millennium requires mainline churches to deal with the trials named by Wuthnow, but also to break their silence on racism and racist nationalism.[2]

In my view, Jesus speaks to us now of the importance of opening the churches' doors to the nation's racially despised and ethnically rejected, who are put at a distance from established conversations.[3] The theology of marginality that called for faith witness among the poor, nameless, and unlearned reflected in the memory of the early Christian communities suggests the God who is with us can most clearly be found by the church that ministers to rejected human beings. What enables people beyond the church compound to see God with us comes from a solidarity that offers justice, life, and complete care for others, especially rejected human beings. Today the barrio is a space for theological discernment and for crossing racial boundaries in order to understand the meaning of the gospel for our society. In the twenty-first century, the witness to Jesus Christ found in the barrio prophetically evangelizes the mainline church by inviting it to the margins where it can enter into the reign of God and work against racial and economic injustices of all kinds.[4]

I believe mainline churches will discover Christ with the beaten-down people of the barrio who believe the gospel is the good news of the kingdom of God that always challenges the abuses of the status quo. Mainline churches that deny themselves by taking up the cross of Jesus Christ will find God fully disclosed in places lacking money, security, and comfort. They will realize that a life worthy of the gospel requires relationship with unwelcome people in a world that needs witnesses to the love and freedom of God. As the mainline church crosses the racial border into the barrio, it shows the world that living the gospel means affirming diversity and celebrating God's Spirit that falls on "every nation under heaven" (Acts 2:5). For the barrio, the good news of the God who is deeply interested in life is that Jesus offers salvation to voiceless people who struggle for economic justice and human dignity as well as repentant people who long to be liberated from loveless forces in their world.

From the perspective of people in the barrio whose historical experience and Christian memory is erased by myths of prosperity and the values represented by the Christology of the dominant culture, social reality is debilitating poverty, discrimination, frustration, despair, oppression, and insecurity. In the barrio, communicating the good news of God means working against the bad news typified by a depressed economy; inadequate public education, health care, and housing; increasing gang and drug-related violence and juvenile crime; the AIDS epidemic; urban capital disinvestment; lack of legal services for immigrants; growing racial and ethnic tensions; and expanding poverty. Barrio people ask the mainline church, Where is mercy, where is justice, where are the pure in heart willing to walk with those on the margins of life? Although the Latino cup of racial humiliation and economic exploitation runs over, few mainline churches make room for the least and vulnerable around them.

As barrio people face the experience of living like rejected outsiders in American society, they engage in struggles to be admitted into the broader debates about national identity. Regrettably, mainline churches have not been deeply engaged in the wider social debate over who is and is not an American and who can and cannot count himself or herself as a member of the national community. As national identity debates in America unfold in an atmosphere of social conflict, deeper issues surface, revealing how the politics of race in America is being turned upside down by Latinos, whose rapidly growing presence calls for rethinking talk about race, poverty, marginality, and civil rights. The dominant myths of society equate the problems of oppression and poverty with the African American community; however, Latinos who have cried out against this view for years are showing how such a narrow perspective constitutes a blinding bias against the multiracial character of U.S. society.

How do Latinos and communities of color other than African American enter the larger context of the politics of race and national identity in the United States? In an essay entitled "The Politics of Recognition," Charles Taylor suggests that "nonrecognition or misrecognition can inflict harm, can be a form of oppression, imprisoning someone in a false, distorted, and reduced mode of being."[5] Latinos especially wish to be seen both as human beings and cultural agents in the United States with a deep past, yet they are persistently either misrecognized or rendered invisible. In his book *Race Matters*, Cornel West reflects an epistemological blindness when he assumes America is essentially a black and white society. West lives and works in a multiracial America, but he overlooks subject matter that lies outside the black/white paradigm of race relations:

> We confine discussions about race in America to the "problems" black people pose for whites rather than consider what this way of viewing black people reveals about us as a nation. . . . Both [liberals and conservatives] fail to see that the presence and predicaments of black people are neither additions to nor defections from American life, but rather constitutive elements of that life.[6]

West's statement about race relations holds true for Latinos, Native Americans, and Asians; indeed, we are all constitutive elements of American life.[7]

Most people known in the United States today as "Hispanic" or "Latino" are immigrants, or descendants of immigrants, from the former colonies of the Spanish Empire of North America, Latin America, and the Caribbean. Today Latinos in the United States represent 12.5 percent of the American population, or an estimated 35 million persons. In other words, the Latino population now represents the country's largest community of color.[8] More than three-quarters of Latinos are native-born or legal residents of the United States. Moreover, U.S. and Latin American countries interact in ways that make Latinos address such diverse issues as the 1994 Chiapas uprising, the effects of NAFTA and CAFTA, Proposition 187, the end of Central America's civil wars, new conditions of border crossings and their policing, and shifts in refugee and immigration law and their effects on Latino civil and human rights.[9]

Although Latinos have been in what is now called the United States since before the Mayflower landed, most have been incorporated following U.S. wars of territorial conquest or have arrived from nations that have historically experienced the negative impact of U.S. capital on their development, or in consequence of U.S. military intervention, overthrow, or undermining of Latin American governments. The history of Latinos disproves the absurd idea of the dominant society that pictures us as temporary strangers or fools from banana republics governed by dictators and supported by drugs. Although Latinos have for centuries been a part of U.S. society, Latino social experience reveals a story of exploitation, discrimination, and inequality. Today, research on Latinos in the United States shows Latino poverty exceeds that of the African American community. In part, the high rate of poverty is attributable to the low-paying jobs held by Latinos and lower rates of educational achievement. Indeed, Latinos have the highest high school dropout rate in the nation.[10]

Since the Civil War, racial oppression and national identity have been understood in the United States in terms of a biracial frame of reference. In contrast, the war against Spain, Mexico, and hundreds of Native American nations on this continent did not result in thinking about national identity and oppression in multiracial terms. Public intellectuals who speak of race only in black and white should cringe before their self-induced blindness. Latinos, Asians, and Native Americans, who have largely been present in the mind of America as obstacles to progress, citizen strangers, or tragic victims, reject being made invisible. In particular, Latinos especially declare that the most honest and useful way to discuss the politics of race in U.S. society is based on a multiracial reading of it.

Latinos know that in this nation of different languages, cultures, and bloodlines what will make living peacefully with our differences possible is a commitment to cross-cultural and racial borders for the sake of a more perfect union. For theological communities, this means that bearing witness to Christ from the color line to the borderline will need to address a growing climate of racism and racist nationalism. If we hope to understand ourselves and others as human beings in all our diversity, we will need to imagine the end of the racial system and a new future life together. In our escapist culture where people shop in climate-controlled malls and watch wars on television while shedding few tears for the dead, mainline Christians will need to heighten their sense of reality at every level of life, but especially in terms of the politics of race.[11]

Throughout this book I will use "race" and "ethnicity" to discuss the way boundaries are marked in American society to distinguish between one group and another. For purposes of clarity, I understand "race" to refer to a social grouping marked by what are perceived to be biologically inherited traits or physical characteristics. "Ethnicity" refers to a social grouping with traits that are culturally inherited, such as language, religion, and/or social practices. The cultural and linguistic differences that bind Latinos into ethnic social groupings are here understood from the perspective of their association with the American construct of racial identity. I will discuss the American biracial frame of reference as an ideological lens that glosses over the racial and ethnic diversity of the Latino community and other populations of color.

ASPECTS OF RACIAL VIOLENCE

In 1900, when W. E. B. DuBois said that "the problem of the twentieth century is the problem of the color line," he was referring to more than black and white Americans. The color line in the United States these days is typified by hostility toward those of any minority group deemed outsiders. I will never forget the report of white students attacking a home of Asian Indian immigrants in Staten Island, smearing the house with paint, and writing on the driveway, "Indians go home. Leave or die." In Houston, white skinheads beat and killed a Vietnamese teenager who cried out just before he died, "God forgive me for coming to this country." Several years ago, in Laurel, Maryland, a group of African American youths stomped a Salvadoran man to death. Then again, just three years before the close of the twentieth century, in Fayettesville, North Carolina, a black couple was murdered by skinheads while out walking one evening.

How were stories of God's saving action preached in churches when in California, Buford Furrow, a white supremacist, burst into the lobby of a Jewish community center and fired seventy shots with a submachine gun before fleeing? How was the gospel preached in mainline churches when the evening news reported that in Chicago, a gunman motivated by racial hate went on a shooting rampage and killed African American basketball coach Ricky Byrdsong shortly after shooting six Orthodox Jewish men walking home from Sabbath services? What kind of Independence Day was the country celebrating when one July 4 in Bloomington, Indiana, Won-Jon Yoon, a twenty-six-year-old Korean graduate student, was killed in front of his church in a drive-by shooting?

There are no signs now blocking the entrance of blacks and Latinos to cafes and theaters. It is also unlikely today that an all-white jury will determine the fate of brown-skinned people, but on a spring day in 1990, in San Diego, California, Dwight Pannel went to a place along the border with two friends, after drinking and popping pills in a suburban home, to kill Latinos. He pulled out a high-powered rifle and shot twelve-year-old Emilio Jimenez Bejinez, who was then crossing the border with his uncle. The young boy was killed instantly, but the white murderer Dwight Pannel—who pleaded guilty to the lesser charge of manslaughter—was sentenced to just two years in jail. What kind of message is being sent when a young white man can kill an innocent undocumented Mexican boy and not be charged with murder?

More recently, in the days immediately following the terrorist attacks on the World Trade Center and the Pentagon, throughout the country Muslims and others mistaken for Middle Eastern reported incidents of anti-Muslim and anti-Arab violence, harassment, and death. In one incident, a false rumor circulated that Muslims in Paterson, New Jersey, had staged a celebratory demonstration and rioted in a city neighborhood after the World Trade Center attack. What all these incidents share in common is the way race fundamentally affects the thought, behavior, and experience of individuals and groups in American society. In other words, race matters and makes a difference in the life of more than just one or two groups in American society.[12]

Arguably, there has been a worldwide challenge to the idea of white supremacy in the post–World War II period in such events as third-world decolonization movements, civil rights movements, and the end of official apartheid in South Africa; nonetheless, we are not now living in a postracial world.[13] Sociologist Howard Winant remarks that in America "it has not been possible to overthrow the deeply rooted belief that the United States is still, as the phrase goes, a 'white man's country.' It has not been possible fully to transform the social, political, economic, and cultural institutions that afford systemic privileges to whites."[14] As racial hate crimes have increased in American society, mainline churches have moved slowly to demonstrate a faith witness consistent with the God of the exodus and of Jesus Christ, who knows the pain of the racially humiliated and despised.

In the development of American society, the link between racial meaning and social structures reveals how the logic of race informs understandings of national identity, human diversity, economic justice, political empowerment, and ideas of democracy. Indeed, in the modern world of the Americas that has evolved over the last five hundred years, racism has permeated "all social identities, cultural forms, and systems of signification."[15] It was only in the past few centuries, under the tutelage of European imperialism, that people in the world began to be racially classified. Moreover, the racial system that gave rise to the world known to us was shaped and maintained by religion, science, philosophy, and politics.[16] As racist discourse unfolded with Western rationalism, white Christians learned to largely ignore that "from one ancestor [God] made all nations" (Acts 17:26).

Race has nothing to do with objective biological reality: instead, it is a cultural product shaped and amended by history. In the history of the modern world its familiar meaning likely began at the end of the Middle Ages, especially rehearsed by the anti-Islamic and anti-Jewish crusades in Spain. Racism represents a deeply distorted view of the unity of humankind implied in the understanding of the parenthood of God and the kinship of all people. As a cultural invention, the concept of race signifies sociopolitical conflicts and interests in reference to perceived differences in physical appearance. Tragically, the belief in a global racial hierarchy led to the violent dispossessing of indigenous people, the kidnapping of Africans for slavery, and the committing of genocide. Observing the role of racism in the process of American nation building, capital development, and labor dynamics, Howard Winant remarks:

> The subjugation of the Americas and the enslavement of Africa financed the rise of the European empires. . . . Vast flows of treasure were shipped to Europe; millions came under the lash of planters and mine-owners. . . . The transition to an integrated, global society with an increasingly complex division of labor demanded the creation of a worldwide racial division between Europe and the "others."[17]

Racism conveys the belief in the inherent superiority of a particular race and its right to domination over others. As Ruth Benedict noted long ago, racism is "the dogma that one ethnic group is condemned by nature to hereditary inferiority and another group is destined to hereditary superiority. It is the dogma that the hope of civilization depends upon eliminating some races and keeping others pure. It is the dogma that one race has carried progress through human history and can alone ensure future progress."[18] One legacy of the Enlightenment was faith in progress, or the myth of cumulative development, thought to underwrite Western culture, but the philosophical justifications of this system of life were based on racist interpretations of history. As Winant observes, "The great philosophers and statesmen of the 18th and 19th centuries, from Kant to Hume to Jefferson and Napoleon, all endorsed the hierarchical division of humanity into superior and inferior races."[19]

In the mid-nineteenth century white superiority was the common explanation given for Europe's growing global domination. At the time W. E. B. DuBois observed the problem of the color line, the idea of race had created an elaborate system of social philosophy and historical interpretation that promoted white supremacy. It was not uncommon for historians to interpret the

inequality of conditions between white and nonwhite humans as the fundamental product of the innate superiority of whites and the natural inferiority
of nonwhites. American anthropologist Daniel Brinton, English historian
Herbert Spencer, American historian Francis Parkman, German philosopher
G. W. F. Hegel, and American clergyman Josiah Strong reflect how history
science, philosophy, religion, and the church were enlisted to legitimate white
supremacy.[20] The Age of Reason was flawed with racist pride, evidenced in
words written by the English philosopher David Hume:

> I am apt to suspect the Negroes and in general all other species of men
> (for there are four or five different kinds) to be inferior to whites. There
> never was a civilized nation of any other complexion than white, nor
> even any individual eminent either in action or speculation.[21]

A popular book written by John Van Evrie, *White Supremacy and Negro Subordination* (1861), is quite interesting in this same vein. For Van Evrie, whites,
who he believed displayed the attributes of "progress" and "indefinite perfectibility," affected the evolution of ancient Central and South American societies. He makes his case by arguing that the foundations of the cultural
achievements of Mexico, Guatemala, Yucatan, and Peru are attributable to
white adventurers or shipwrecked sailors. He also says that leaders in Asia such
as Attila the Hun, Genghis Khan, Tamerline, and Confucius were actually
"pure" whites. Social advances in Africa were also due to the process of white
admixture with the African ruling class. In other words, white people are not
only superior to any people of color wherever they are found, but they are the
source of all great civilizations.[22]

William Appess, a member of the Pequot nation who became a Methodist
pastor, published *An Indian's Looking Glass for the White Man* (1833). This work
attempted to correct the racist views held by whites about Native Americans
and other nonwhite social groups. He wrote, "If Black or Red skins, or any
other skin color is disgraceful to God, it appears God has disgraced himself a
great deal—for he has made fifteen colored people to one white, and placed
them on the earth."[23] Appess questioned the theological views of Americans
who hold God captive to racist interpretations of human difference, which justified the theft of a continent, the murder of indigenous women and children,
and the negation of Native American human rights. Appess reminded the
white church that racism is the deepest form of alienation from God, especially since God is the creator and racism assumes a defect in God's creative
action.

The U.S. racial order powered by an epistemology driven by ranked differences between white and nonwhite human beings was deeply challenged by

the Civil War and the Reconstruction period. Still, by the 1880s, Jim Crow laws emerged that separated white and black persons in public accommodations, transportation, housing, schools, and in the workplace. Moreover, blacks were regulated by violent racist organizations such as the Ku Klux Klan, mob violence, and lack of law enforcement by state agencies.[24] African Americans migrated from the rural South to southern and northern urban centers and developed political organizations and movements to challenge the racial order.

For instance, the Harlem Renaissance issued forth in the production of music, literature, and art that asserted black Americans' resistance to segregation and the racist social order. Arguably, a factor leading to the civil rights struggle of the 1950s and 1960s was the growing political awareness of African Americans who saw the contradiction between freedom fighting in World War II and the lack of it at home. Black soldiers back from war claimed the idea that either all human beings are made in the image of God, or none are. African Americans who fought for Jewish freedom overseas confronted the evil of racism at home in social actions that envisioned a world of freedom for all humanity. As Martin Luther King Jr. remarked at the National Conference of Religion and Race in 1963:

> We will not seek to rise from a position of disadvantage to one of advantage, thus subverting justice. Nor will we seek to substitute one tyranny for another. We will be imbued with the conviction that a philosophy of black supremacy is as injurious as a philosophy of white supremacy. God is not interested merely in the freedom of black men, and brown men, and yellow men; God is interested in the freedom of the whole human race—the creation of a society in which all men appreciate the dignity and worth of the individual.[25]

The post–World War II period and the civil rights movement saw an intensely sustained antiracist movement develop by other defined racial groups such as Native Americans, Asians Americans, and Latinos that refocused the meaning of democracy and American national identity. The lessons learned from the African American civil rights movement resulted in civic organizations mobilizing around antiracist strategies of empowerment in legislative, judicial, workplace, and grassroots community contexts. As the United States moved to assume a position of definitive global power, racial justice movements called into question fundamental matters of justice, equality, freedom, and democracy within it. Racial justice movements struggled to show America and even the church the error of dividing people into such categories as race.

Because most Asians have immigrated to the United States since the 1960s, they do not share the common history of exploitation and racial humiliation experienced by people of Chinese, Filipino, or Japanese ancestry. Japanese Americans who were placed in concentration camps throughout the United States during World War II experienced one of the most blatant violations of civil rights in modern American history. For Japanese Americans, World War II was not the so-called good war where the heroes and villains were obvious. Some 120,000 Japanese Americans were sent to camps in the aftermath of Pearl Harbor in a roundup authorized by Franklin Roosevelt's Executive Order 9066. Secretary of the Interior Harold Ickes wrote to the president:

> Crowded into cars like cattle, these hapless people were hurried away to hastily constructed and thoroughly inadequate concentration camps, with soldiers with nervous muskets on guard, in the great American desert. We gave the fancy name of "relocation centers" to these dust bowls, but they were concentration camps nonetheless, although not as bad as Dachau or Buchenwald. War-excited imaginations, raw race-prejudice and crass greed kept hateful public opinion along the Pacific Coast at fever heat.[26]

Meanwhile, domestic labor demands were met by the U.S. government after reaching an agreement with Mexico in 1942 known as the Bracero Program. Although it called for protection against discrimination, in actuality Mexicans who were allowed to enter the country to work were left unprotected, and they suffered poor nutrition, excessive charges for housing, racial discrimination, ill treatment, and exposure to dangerous chemicals. Growers were provided with cheap labor, and the U. S. government was able to enlist more Mexican Americans to fight in the war. Like African Americans, Mexican American soldiers faced blatant racism once they returned home from combat.[27] For instance, Sergeants José Mendoza Lopez and Macario García, recipients of the Congressional Medal of Honor, were barred like other Latinos and blacks from eating at white restaurants. War heroes such as Felix Longoria were refused burial services from funeral parlors serving whites.[28]

The historical sociology of race in America requires that serious attention be given to the changing semantic field of racist ideology. For instance, today's racism is characterized by white avoidance of direct hostility toward defined racial groups, affirmation of the principles of equal opportunity and egalitarianism, but rejection of programs to amend racial inequality and economic injustices. This new politics of race represents whites as victims of racial inequality, thus removing from race analysis "the social gravity of poverty, economic exploitation and class divisions."[29] What should disturb the mainline church today is not the resurgence of racial hatred and right-wing groups in America, but the apparent silence of the church in the face of it.

Today the United States is no less a separate and broken society, but we are more acutely aware that the dividing walls of hostility reflect tensions in more than black and white. The problem of the borderline has raised its head in the form of racism against immigrants of color. In American society mainline churches must not only stand boldly against the racist system, but they must seek to evangelize society by contributing to the formation of a new civil rights framework that opposes the violation of the civil and human rights of immigrants. As the mainline church seeks to draw society closer to the One who always offers life before death, it must address the racism that erects barriers against creating a society based on equality and inclusion of citizens and noncitizens alike. Let us now examine the racism that is directed toward immigrants of color, especially Latinos.

THE PROBLEM OF THE BORDERLINE

The growth of immigrant communities of color in major metropolitan areas has sparked great insecurity among some white Americans, giving rise to a desire to especially restrict, exclude, and attack immigrants. In the post–September 11 world, a growing number of Americans of European descent equate the growing racial ethnic pluralism of the country with trouble and danger.[30] Although America remains more open to foreigners than other countries, immigrants of color are too easily associated in the minds of many Americans with terrorism, lawlessness, and unwanted problems. Ironically, as mainline churches argue over the value of multicultural congregations and evangelizing immigrant newcomers, conservative groups' rhetoric of exclusion fuels ethnic violence, the racialization of what it means to be an American, and the idea that true Americans are white.

Since the 1990s, white resentment has been especially sparked by the growing visibility of newcomers speaking Spanish in the public square, Muslims building mosques in major urban areas, and Koreans, Arabs, Latinos, Indians, and persons from other ethnic communities of color owning businesses with signs in languages other than English.[31] This resentment led to white conservative efforts to propose laws to deny dark-skinned newcomers the right to give birth to citizens. Birthright citizenship is guaranteed by the Fourteenth Amendment, whose provision was enacted to ensure the citizenship rights of freed slaves. Legal scholar Ian Haney Lopez remarked of the efforts to repeal the existing citizenship clause of the Fourteenth Amendment:

SUSPECTS

I woke up this
morning feeling
sick about America

and picked up the
telephone to call
the equal opportunity

office in the nation's
capital responsible
for writing us out

of history. America
why do you hang a threat
over our heads like daily bread

and keep us in the shadows
cooking, cleaning, and
caring for your children?

America why do you suspect
us on our own land and watch
us with deep disturbed eyes

on every corner and along
the border from houses we
built in this place we named?

America look deep to
find those dreams cast
aside and see my face.

> This proposal implicitly discriminates along racial lines. The effort to
> deny citizenship to children born here to undocumented immigrants
> seems to be motivated not by an abstract concern over the political sta-
> tus of parents, but by racial animosity against Asians and Latinos,
> those commonly seen as comprising the vast bulk of undocumented
> migrants.[32]

The civil rights era led communities of color to demand equal rights and political inclusion. Today the experience of Latinos suggests the need to rethink
the meaning of civil rights and inclusion based on protection against future
biases and historic discrimination.[33]

The United States is in the midst of a Second Great Wave of immigration,
which some researchers attribute to years of economic expansion and others
to the liberal provisions of the Immigration Act (1965). Because recent immigrants have come from predominantly non-European societies, some Americans fear this new wave threatens democracy, linguistic unity, and the tradition
of Anglo-Saxon Protestant culture. Historically, immigration has been dominated by certain regions for periods of time, and over the last four-and-a half
decades the dominant sending region has been Latin America. Today there are
far more Americans who feel Latinos drain public funds and culturally divide
America than there are persons who think Latinos reinvigorate America's
work ethic and add diversity to an American culture that values it.

The American racial framework of otherness—which accented cultural and
physical differences—resulted in an unfavorable context that met the massive
waves of southern and eastern Europeans and smaller flow of Asians that
arrived during the so-called First Great Wave of immigration (1890–1920).
Although these immigrant groups were largely economically and politically
powerless, they were not immune from anti-immigrant agitation or being
denounced as either radicals or of inferior stock.[34] One researcher observes
that without a white nativist movement during the First Great Wave of immigration the Chinese Exclusion Act (1882), an anti-Japanese Gentleman's
Agreement (1908), and a series of restrictive acts (1917–1924) targeting eastern and southern Europeans would not have been seen.[35]

Interestingly, when eastern and southern Europeans arrived in America
some northern European nativists were concerned about their racial impact
on society. In his book *The Passing of the Great Race* (1916), eugenicist Madison Grant extolled the superior qualities of Nordic Europeans and warned of
their destruction through intermixture with blacks and inferior Europeans in
America. For Madison Grant, racial mixing with black and inferior Europeans
was a social crime that would lead America toward "racial suicide" and the
eventual disappearance of Nordic white civilization. In time, southern and
eastern European immigrants were reclassified to become white and assimi-

lated into the mainstream American culture.[36] Today's immigrants, and the perception of racial difference on the part of the host society, come into a highly charged racist-nationalist environment that contributes to deeper inequalities.

Racist-nationalists now want to close the border, arguing that Latino immigrants pose a threat to national identity. Their anti-immigrant platform even finds support in the work of liberal historian Arthur Schlesinger Jr., who views multiculturalism as undermining the uniform public identity allegedly needed in a democratic society. In his book *The Disuniting of America*, Schlesinger underestimates how America was divided by race, sex, gender, and religion by suggesting the American experience of national identity is defined by a linear process of social integration.[37] The American quest for empire was fueled by a racist doctrine of Manifest Destiny that deformed ethnic relations and subverted the pursuit of a common national identity. In the beginning, the U.S. constitution declared that citizens were white men of property, with exclusions based on class, race, and gender.[38]

Today Americans who are afraid of the new complexion of immigrants seek a white future for the nation. A National Defense University report, *Security in the Americas*, echoes the fear that Latinos will decompose U.S. cultural institutions and introduce chaos in the country's internal self-understanding of national identity.[39] The report represents Latinos as a "nation within the nation" that poses a threat that needs to be controlled, which can best be achieved through restrictive immigration policies, the elimination of bilingual education funds, dismemberment of social welfare programs, and support for such measures as Proposition 187.[40] The growth of overwhelmingly poor, exploited, and vulnerable Latino immigrant communities does not call up images of loving the stranger; instead, it promotes the idea of national defense.

Perhaps no other state in the union has revealed racist nationalism at work as California has done in recent years. In 1994, a majority of white (83 percent) and African American (55 percent) voters in California overwhelmingly passed Proposition 187 to "save their state from Latinos."[41] Proposition 187 intended to prevent so-called illegal immigration and to punish the mostly undocumented Mexicans, Salvadorans, and Guatemalans in the state who, as Harold Ezzell, a one-time high-level official of the INS and later a supporter of Proposition 187 once remarked, needed to be "caught, skinned and fried."[42] It severely restricts access of undocumented immigrants to public services and requires public employees to report them. Many Latinos feared Proposition 187, and many families stopped going to health clinics or withdrew children from school, fearing deportation. One Latino researcher noted that Proposition 187 affirms Andrew Hacker's observation that "a politics purposively permeated by race has consolidated enough white Americans as a self-conscious racial majority. This is not to say that they are bigots or racists. It is rather that they are threatened, not always in ways they understand."[43]

The anti-immigrant sentiment represented by Proposition 187 reflects how new immigrants of color are made scapegoats for problems ranging from the spread of disease to crowded schools and are even being accused of contributing to the extinction of the white race. Latino identity is not constructed by the myth of the United States as a nation of immigrants who become American through the exercise of political rights and civic responsibilities. Instead, Latinos are multiculturalists who must be kept out or subjected to the interests of white racial hegemony. California's racist-nationalists argue that Latino immigrants and citizens will someday conspire to take over the western states and eventually the whole country. Linda B. Hayes, the Proposition 187 media director, made this argument public in a letter to the *New York Times*:

> By flooding the state with 2 million illegal aliens to date, and increasing that figure each of the following ten years, Mexicans in California would number 15 million to 20 million by 2004. During those ten years about 5 million to 8 million Californians would have emigrated to other states. If these trends continued, a Mexico-controlled California could vote to establish Spanish as the sole language of California, 10 million more English-speaking Californians could flee, and there could be a statewide vote to leave the Union and annex California to Mexico.[44]

Anti-Latino groups in California not only feared white racial hegemony and English-language dominance was threatened by the new immigrants to the United States, but they attributed in no uncertain terms the problems of public schools and crime to those "third world" people too. Barbara Coe, a draftee of Proposition 187, used racial imagery to blame public school problems and crime on immigrants:

> You get illegal alien children, Third World children, out of the schools and you will reduce violence. That is a fact. . . . You're not dealing with a lot of shiny faced, little kiddies. . . . You're dealing with Third World cultures who come in, they shoot, they beat, they stab and they spread their drugs around in our school system.[45]

Interestingly, rather than being a social threat or a strain on public services, "all immigrants together earn about $300 billion each year, pay over $70 billion in taxes, and use only $5.7 billion in welfare benefits."[46]

Latinos in all statuses were impacted by Proposition 187. Latino citizens, documented and undocumented alike, who felt attacked marched in Los Angeles in defense of their homes in the barrio, in the name of the people who are always mostly in the ranks of the working poor, in defense of mixed families, and in the name of human rights.[47] Latino men, women, and children protested the action of anti-immigrant groups inspired by the deepest values of Americanism, an exercise of civic nationalism in the context of a radically pluralist society. In part, the California struggle for immigrant and civil rights shows that the exclusionary rhetoric of racist-nationalists reinforces ideas about nationhood that are racially and culturally exclusive. In part, Proposition 187 showed that no other group in the country has its citizenship and legal status questioned as Latinos do.

In his best-selling book *Alien Nation*, the British-born senior editor of *Forbes*, Peter Brimelow, proposes a race-based immigration policy to ensure a white future for the United States. Brimelow, who is no champion of the Voting Rights Act (1965) or the Civil Rights Act (1964), takes aim at the Immigration Act (1965) that eliminated the so-called national origins quotas from U.S. immigrant and national law. He believes passage of the Immigration Act was like shooting a wounded white society after the battle for civil rights was over. The Immigration Act sparked an ethnic and racial transformation of America that threatens the "white ethnic core" of the nation. Brimelow believes this transformation threatens America today even more than did the Civil War or the Cold War:

> For the first time, virtually all immigrants are racially distinct "visible minorities." They come not from Europe, previously the common homeland even for the 1890–1920 immigrants about which Americans were so nervous. Instead, these new immigrants are from completely different, and arguably incompatible, cultural traditions. And, as we have seen, they are coming in such numbers that their impact on America is enormous—inevitably within the foreseeable future, they will transform it.[48]

Common sense reveals to Brimelow that the United States is in peril unlike ever before since the revolution; indeed, the United States may become an "alien nation" because of a dramatic increase in "third world immigration." Therefore, Brimelow offers a raced-based solution to the immigration problem which calls for limiting illegal immigration by doubling the size of the U.S. Border Patrol; sealing the U.S.-Mexico border "with a fence, or a ditch"; reviving Operation Wetback, a mid-1950s mass deportation program; eliminating all public benefits to illegal immigrants, including public education; eliminating amnesty programs for illegal aliens; devising a system to interdict money transfers by illegal aliens to their home country; and repealing the birthright citizenship clause in the Fourteenth Amendment. Because his book especially targets Latinos, he also proposes replacing the census category "Hispanic" with national-origin or racial classifications as appropriate.

Although favoring the admittance of legal immigrants who he says "look like me," Brimelow proposes temporarily stopping or reducing all legal immigration, doing away with special categories such as refugees, eliminating family reunification, and excluding legal immigrants from affirmative action benefits. These measures will help restore the racial and ethnic composition of society prior to 1965, when America was 90 percent white. Brimelow cannot accept the possibility that current demographic shifts may produce a future where no one race is dominant. Of course, Latino and African American urban riots and the civil rights movement show there was a great deal wrong with the nation then. Raoul Contreras remembers society in 1965:

> In their precious 1965, I was 24 years old and, though a veteran of six years service in the American armed forces and a life-long U.S. citizen, I could not vote in some Texas counties. . . . In 1965, Black children were murdered by white males in many ways, in many places, in the South. Black male adults were beaten, killed and castrated in Mississippi, Alabama, Arkansas, and other Southern States for the crime of having black skin. . . . In 1965, though a veteran, college graduate and political professional, a bartender refused to serve me a drink in a Texas bar because, he said, "We don't serve foreigners." That was Brimelow's 1965 America. Unfortunately, it was my America too.[49]

The exclusionary discourse of Brimelow's *Alien Nation* is particularly directed toward the Latino community, which is represented as a "strange anti-nation in the United States" that refuses to Americanize.[50] Brimelow believes surging Hispanic immigration must be stopped in defense of the European common stock of America. Latinos threaten the white racial purity of the nation and are committed to retaining their mother tongue and cultural traditions; thus, American national culture is at risk. Moreover, Latinos—like African Americans and other so-called third-world immigrants—represent crime-prone ethnic cultures. Brimelow believes Latinos and third-world immigrants have driven America's crime rate up; thus, the "new units of organized crime" in America are Mexican, South Korean, Chinese, African, Chaldean, Colombian, and Iraqi.

In Brimelow's racist-nationalist vision of America, the beginning was white and there is no place for new articulations of cultural and ethnic differences. He denies that the term "America" is not qualified by ethnicity; however, political unity and ongoing cultural exchange among many groups are the distinctive marks of our great nation. Not only does the United States have no definable ethnicity, but long before the arrival of eastern and southern Europeans, who made the nation uneasy, it was Latino, African American, and Asian. Racial justice movements have not overcome the legacy of hundreds of years of racial subjugation, economic exploitation, and political repression, but today we are challenged to understand by virtue of coming together the need for social change that affirms ethnic pluralism and the values of justice, freedom, and equality for all.

CONCLUSION

Brimelow believes immigrants of color are worthy of blame for anything that is wrong with America. If Schlesinger overstates the ease with which ethnic differences melted away in American society, Brimelow's racist discourse refuses to admit that American history is dominated by the nation-building interaction of different racial and ethnic groups.[51] This naturalized Englishman's writing found an audience in mainstream culture that does not object to racist discourse and that prefers to surround debates about the problem of the borderline in apocalyptic historical pessimism and covert racist ideology.[52] As a Latino, the greatest challenge I faced reading *Alien Nation* was simply getting through it.

Racist-nationalists such as Brimelow and immigration restrictionists such as the ones supporting Proposition 187 are sending immigrants of color a message that says they have an inferior position in American society. Moreover, the racist discourse of the new nativists fuels anti-immigrant sentiment that often not only precipitates violence against people of color, but enables the denial of privileges to citizens thought to be foreigners.[53] Regrettably, while authors like Brimelow are busy blaming immigrants for any imagined problem, fewer still are stopping to reflect how the flow of immigration from Latin America and third-world countries is tied to U.S. foreign policy, agribusiness, and corporate interests.[54]

Will the problem of the color line and the borderline ever be resolved in America? Will the injustices that accompany the racial system at home and overseas ever be overcome? What will enable immigrant families and their children to overcome the discriminatory barriers that impede their adaptation to American society? If we are to answer these questions, the exercise of political responsibilities and the struggles that continue to expand the meaning of democracy, liberty, social justice, and belonging will need to be strengthened. What is the good news for the enduring American dilemma? The good news is that God in Christ aims to repair broken relationships and disunity in the world. There is no place in God's reign for racism or racist nationalism, especially given the new motivation given to us by God to build life together based on justice, equality, and love.

The problem of the color line and borderline tells us that American Christianity betrays Christ when it clings to the ungodly idea that African Americans, Latinos, Native Americans, and Asians are inferior human beings who threaten the existence of national society. The mainline church will be relevant in our divided world to the extent it links the commitment to loving community to human diversity. Mainline churches have a critical role to play in evangelizing culture toward a vision of society that recognizes that the diverse qualities and characteristics of human beings originate in God's divine being. Rather than keeping silent in the face of racial divisions in American society, mainline churches must more aggressively proclaim the God who crosses all racial and ethnic boundaries and rejects white supremacy and xenophobia.

My examination of salient aspects of our divided world where "death before life" is offered suggests that communicating the good news of God demands bearing witness to Jesus, who offers life before death.[55] In our world apart, Christ calls the church to engage in a prophetic evangelization that tells the story of God's saving actions in the world and works to create the material and social relationships that make Christ present in people who in their luxurious differences reflect the reign of God. Let us now turn to the good news that is erupting from the barrio and consider what it offers the mainline church with respect to its concern to enliven a divided world with the hopeful community, loving relationships, and abundant life offered by Jesus Christ.

THE DEVIL

he saw the devil
busy in the alley,
next to the church
bells, in the living

rooms of bishops and the
rich who prefer noble
lies. he pointed to
the places where life

is evil now, the corners
where sons and daughters
are struck down, the
sidewalks the learned

scholars mistakenly believe
home to the dead. he saw the
devil convincing people to
pray to the God of destructive

greed, the One who creates
all things in grief, and
leaves us with secret pools
of sadness. he watched the

deal-making over the ledge of
the roof that covers the houses
of the poor, confident of
the extraordinary end to this

loveless time, when heaven
will rain flowers from the
darkened sky, to announce
the coming time of our

renewal.

2

Good News from the Barrio

Mainline denominations are currently refocusing attention on the theme of congregational revitalization, especially in light of their evangelizing efforts that promote membership growth. In most cases the motivation for evangelism has little to do with rethinking the meaning of following Jesus and commitment to his message of solidarity, justice, and peace. Church growth defines what evangelism means today, instead of the concern to convey God's reign of justice, peace, and salvation.[1] Church leaders from different denominational bodies promote the idea that the vitality of the church depends on preaching a user-friendly gospel, improving growth-oriented managerial skills, and providing congregational contexts to experience personal spirituality apart from worldly concerns.

For many mainline church leaders, evangelization is often least concerned with how to understand God's option for the world or incarnating the gospel in the struggle against racism, economic exploitation, and openness to others. Conventional approaches to evangelism seem to excite church leaders more about the possibilities of growing megachurches than encouraging persons to follow Christ by becoming themselves good news to the poor in the world for which Christ died. The contemporary church misunderstands evangelism when it simply equates it with promoting church growth instead of following Jesus. Evangelism should keep us close to human suffering for the purpose of discerning and responding to the loving God who frees us from the values of a divided cultural order.

In *Biblical Perspectives on Evangelism*, Walter Brueggemann cautions mainline Christians against withdrawing the radical news of God's rule from the world. Conservatives who reduce the Bible to "confessional safety" and liberals who avoid the radical epistemological challenge of a subversive gospel are equally called to live in the world based on action and witness to God's alternative purposes for creation.[2] Hence, the ultimate concern of Christians is not institutional growth, but the crisis of our shared creation reflected in the threat of nuclear and biological weapons, international debt, terror, greed, interreligious hostility, poverty, and violence.[3] Christians announcing the God who rules should always declare that the world's bad news is of concern to God.

Evangelism became the concern of mainline churches who were faced with declining membership, shrinking budgets, and growing cultural marginalization. Although the logic of church growth is questionable, it is possible to affirm the growth impulse to the extent that its basic theological concern is focused on sharing the gospel message in a secularized and racially separated society. Church leaders ought to feel positively about evangelistic strategies motivated by a Christian concern to address modern Western society's denial of God in human affairs. Modern technological, secular, and pluralistic culture still needs people with the courage to make God's promises known to others. In cultures that resist the message of the gospel and promote the idea that God is dead, evangelism offers a truth that sets people free (see John 8:31).[4]

Mainline churches need to let go of their survival mentality to more aggressively proclaim the hope of the gospel. In our time of insecurity and rising global conflicts, Christians who have a living sense of faith will find renewal for the church by working for a new earth in radical obedience to the God who requires them to see the truth about social reality. Acting on the deepest values of faith means not plotting numerical growth but focusing more of our energies on a witness that proclaims good news in a world overwhelmed with poverty, oppression, injustice, and death. The hostility on the part of many people in modern culture toward the church is far less threatening to the future of Christianity than the rejection that comes from people who decide the gospel represented by mainline churches does not bring hope to situations of despair or the experience of being a reconciled people of God.

Church leaders typically pursue evangelism plans focused on the verbal proclamation of the gospel, because they believe this is the best way to express the Great Commission, "Go therefore and make disciples of all nations" (Matt. 28:19). Pastors and lay leaders across various denominations are upset by how the wider culture leads their members away from church, while some argue that the membership decline of mainline churches is attributable to a diminished sense of personal faith in Jesus.[5] I think indifference to the mainline church results from a failure to connect the Great Commission to the Great Commandment: "Love one another as I have loved you" (John 15:12).

Christians who connect these two directives will more fully embody a discipleship in Christ open to new ways of thinking, seeing, and doing.[6]

Because evangelism is far more than working for church growth, it requires rediscovering Christ's prophetic ministry and its value for an unjustly structured world. In a world of massive and intolerable levels of suffering caused by poverty, institutionalized violence, and systems of power that crush human beings, evangelism is activity that empowers Christians to stand before God without indifference toward the misery of the poor or talk that blames them for their condition. Evangelism should enable the church to use God's word of truth to prophetically face oppressive structures such as consumerism, militarism, the world economic order, racism, sexism, and classism.[7] Thus, following Christ includes speaking the truth that sets us free by living in the presence of the crucified One in the life of the racially despised, hungry, thirsty, abused, and powerless.

Christians who define evangelism as a church-multiplying activity or simply a personal affirmation of faith in Jesus Christ need to think more deeply about what it means to emerge from a history of darkness into God's light (1 Pet. 2:9); indeed, the communication of the gospel in the world of the poor, the unaccomplished, and the self-centered requires careful theological reflection. Evangelism is centered in Jesus Christ and offers a message that moves people to respond to God's love in a variety of human contexts. Evangelism announces the coming reign of God from a historical point of departure at the periphery of society and all those places where social nobodies tirelessly wait for good news from God. Orlando Costas made this observation about such a prophetic stance on evangelization:

> If evangelization starts on the periphery of society, if it works from the bottom up, the good news of God's kingdom is visibly demonstrated and credibly announced as a message of liberation, love, justice, and peace. When the gospel makes "somebody" out of the "nobodies" of society, when it restores the self-worth of the marginalized, when it enables the oppressed to have reason for hope, when it empowers the poor to struggle and suffer for justice and peace, then it is truly good news of a new life—the saving power of God (Rom 1:16).[8]

As we begin to explore the meaning of evangelization for a divided world, it helps to note the word derives from the Greek *euangelion*, which means "good news" or "good message." The good news of God is embedded in the idea of God's universal reign expressed in Isaiah: "How beautiful upon the mountains are the feet of the messenger who announces peace, who brings good news, who announces salvation, who says to Zion, 'Your God reigns'" (Isa. 52:7; cf. Ps. 96). For Christians this good news is Jesus Christ, who

preached God's reign and who identified himself with the poor, rejected, bro-
kenhearted, and captive (Luke 4:16–21). In what follows, I argue that the good
news of Jesus Christ requires a prophetic imagination that makes the church
present in mission and in the suffering of the least members of society.[9]

PROPHETIC IMAGINATION

Today the middle-class captivity of the church often results in a lack of concern for the rich collection of prophetic material describing God's preferential love for the excluded. Middle-class congregations too easily overlook the
prophetic passion for social justice, which centers attention on the situation of
the poor. The problems of the poor and racial minorities in American society
today mostly command polite conversation but not practical concern.[10] Meanwhile, Jesus' name is even associated with white supremacist groups, right-
wing politics, and an affluence that contributes to greater social divisions.[11]
Mainline churches open to the agonies and struggles of the barrio will awaken
to the prophetic call of Christ and realize that the historical Jesus was "not just
a thinker with ideas but a rebel with a cause. . . . [He was] the embodied
Galilean who lived a life of divine justice in an unjust world."[12]

How should Christians today share the good news that God is conquering
the forces acting against God? Can mainline congregations claim a public
voice in terms of the truth affirmed in the passion of Christ rather than
remaining obsessed with questions of meaning and purpose? What will keep
Christians from accommodating the gospel to the life-denying values of a
dominant culture harmful to the poor and racially excluded? What will inspire
mainline congregations to favor a practice of faith open to the life in the experience of rejected people? When will preaching about a gospel of personal salvation be linked to concerns of structural redemption? The church does not
have to grope around for alternative theoretical understandings of the meaning of God to find answers to these questions; instead, such answers can be
found in the church's "prophetic imagination," which graciously reveals what
God promises to do in the world.

Mainline churches can reopen congregational culture by developing a
prophetic imagination that leads to a ministry that evokes a "consciousness
and perception alternative to the consciousness and perception of the dominant culture around us."[13] God empowers Christians to imagine a way of life
alternative to that upheld by a controlling culture that is deaf to the cry of the
poor and blind to the racially humiliated, who display the ongoing passion of
Christ in the world. The prophetic imagination begins with nothing less than
people guided by faith in God to create social, political, economic, and cul-

tural institutions and practices that map a new road toward a different future for society. As a principle of evangelism, the prophetic imagination leads congregations to engage in activities that promote compassionate action in place of accommodating theologies that legitimate systems of oppression and economic injustice.

But what is a prophet? What is prophetic action? Popular Christian thinking often defines a prophet as an individual who serves God by predicting the future; however, biblical prophets do not predict future events like fortune-tellers. In light of the memory of God's saving action and the radical hope in life transformed by the activity of justice, biblical prophets criticized the established order and energized persons and communities to face a new future. The good news of God they announced called on people to act now for or against God's ultimate will for humanity.[14] Biblical prophets concerned themselves with God's future overrunning the present and a return to the central claims of faith embedded in God's merciful love and justice. Thus, the prophets inspire faith in the God who is intolerant of injustice and who prepares a banquet for all people (Isa. 25:6).

People filled with a desire to know and do the will of God in their lives best reflect the prophetic imagination in a world that struggles with injustice. The prophetic imagination leads Christians to express oppositional discourse and action in a society that idolizes wealth, power, and possessions. As Christians embody the prophetic word, they become more aware that God is responsive to the concerns of the poor and those who suffer unjustly at the hands of others. In this regard, prophetic faith understands God is working to establish justice in the economic, political, social, and cultural system, and toward correcting the conduct of the powerful who squeeze life out of the poor and rejected of society. A prophetic imagination results in evangelizing approaches that affirm that in the midst of hunger, poverty, doubt, and desperation God offers hope and the renewal of life.

The interpreted Word of God in the writings of the biblical prophets varied, but not one of the prophets bore witness to faith in the clouds. They courageously stayed within reality by criticizing abuses of power and turning away from God. They spoke of God's love, righteousness, purpose, suffering, and obedience in light of God's option for the oppressed and poor. For the prophets, religion was not an opiate, but part of the daily good news that is written through the struggles and hopes of persons who love kindness and mercy. The biblical prophets struggled to have belief and behavior reflect God's different vision for social reality. Their criticism of religious and political leaders helps us to see today what is meant by prophetic faith and how to approach evangelism committed to social justice.

The prophets faced turbulent events in their day. They spoke of the God of justice who gathers up the shattered community, who pays close attention to the cries of the poor, and who guides people walking in darkness toward light (Isa. 9:2). They rejected the widespread problem in American society today that associates ultimate meaning with high social status, material possessions, and limited social commitments defined by racism and nationalism. The suffering of the poor grieved the heart of the prophets, who refused to reconcile the idea of salvation with piling up wealth and privileges. The narrative description of prophetic actions appeals to our imagination today and helps us image the God of saving justice who gives sight to the blind and promises a future where "water shall break forth in the wilderness, and streams in the desert" (Isa. 35:6).[15]

Biblical prophets such as Isaiah, Amos, Jeremiah, and Micah reveal God to us from below in the history of those who suffer unjustly, are economically exploited, and experience life so torn apart they often cannot speak. Although the prophetic literature constitutes about one-fourth of the Old Testament, well-off Christians show a great deal of skill in ignoring the prophetic call to treat the poor with the same kindness shown to them by God (Exod. 22:21–24; Deut. 15:13–15; John 3:16; 2 Cor. 8:9). Mainline churches that unfold their prophetic imagination will more fully relate faith to the existential reality of the poor, will welcome strangers into the body of Christ, and will pursue peace in a divided and violent world.

According to the prophets, saving justice means that God requires us to light up the darkness in the world, not just to sing it up in worship. To be sure, biblical prophets were critical of worship experiences that lacked good news. Isaiah, for instance, tells us that God despises worship and rituals performed by those who oppress others (Isa. 58:3–7). Amos, a herder and caretaker of sycamore trees, attacks the upper classes who mixed worship and oppression of the poor (Amos 5:21–24). Jeremiah makes it clear that God is absent from worship where there is no commitment to the rights of the poor (Jer. 1:1–7).[16] In short, the abiding love of God is present when the people of God defend the poor and uphold justice against the powers of greed and oppression. God wants Christians to show their love for beaten-down people by working in the world to bring about the justice and solidarity that will disserve the brutalizing interests of mammon.

In short, the prophets engaged neither in philosophical speculation regarding the existence of God nor systematic reflection on God's relationship to the social and physical environment.[17] Quite simply, knowledge of God for the prophets was associated with doing justice to the poor and the oppressed. They point a finger at those responsible for the social injustice suffered by the poor and those the social structure pushes continually to the edges of society. As Gustavo Gutierrez notes:

The prophets condemn every kind of abuse, every form of keeping the poor in poverty or of creating new poor people. . . . The finger is pointed at those who are to blame. Fraudulent commerce and exploitation are condemned (Hos. 12:8; Amos 8:5; Mic. 6:10–11; Isa. 3:14; Jer. 5:27; 6:12), as well as the hoarding of lands (Mic. 2:1–3; Ezek. 22:29; Hab. 2:5–6), dishonest courts (Amos 5:7; Jer. 22:13–17; Mic. 3:9–11; Isa. 5:23; 10:1–2), the violence of the ruling classes (2 Kgs 23:30, 35; Amos 4:1; Mic. 3:1–2; 6:12; Jer. 23:13–17), slavery (Neh. 5:1–5; Amos 2:6; 8:6), unjust taxes (Amos 4:1; 5:11–12), and unjust functionaries (Amos 5:7; Jer. 5:28).[18]

The prophets tirelessly showed that God cares about the poor, whose lives are made bitter by exploitation and shortened by hard service.

Mainline congregations need to more rigorously cultivate their prophetic imagination to understand God's universal love reaching out to all humanity from the world of marginality. The prophetic imagination will enable us to feel both the pain of those whose life is merely a time between suffering and death as well as shame for the world that produced it. The prophetic vision of justice and solidarity commits the church to the evangelistic task of redefining the context of God in the reality of those who cry out to heaven for the right to live.[19] The prophetic imagination will permit us to discover the depth of evangelism in contexts otherwise ignored. In this sense, the march to the edges of society is a step toward beginning the prophetic project of turning swords into plowshares and cultivating a way of life free from unjust stress, premature death, and economic exploitation (Isa. 65:17–25).

THE REJECTED

In mainstream America the poor are largely treated with suspicion and scorn; however, in the Scriptures God defends the poor, the widow, the orphan, the excluded, and the stranger. In the Beatitudes Jesus blesses the poor (Luke 6:20–22). The poor, who are disproportionately represented among people of color, threaten the myth of American success that equates hard work, the avoidance of idleness, frugality, and good management of resources with economic prosperity and upward mobility.[20] In middle-class mainline congregations in various parts of the country, I have heard conversations where the poor are discussed as "those people" unworthy of help and who only deserve criticism to correct character deficiencies and dependent behavior. Because the prevailing cultural view is that poverty is an individual problem, more negative moral judgments about the poor get expressed in congregations than analyses of poverty in larger systemic contexts. I have rarely heard the view

CITY ROOF

on a similar day the
workers looked to heaven
for a sign to indulge
their conscience with
planetary things, they
looked at the street
from the old church roof
and saw heaven escaping
the poverty below, they
hankered for a hymn to
set things right but
the sounds in the air
left them bare, they went
back to work not to think
of the misery on the block,
a clear light filled them
and they sang with the genius
of God: We Shall Overcome!

expressed that the gospel directs the church to see the poor as persons for whom Jesus Christ is good news.

The plight of the poor raises questions about justice when incredible affluence unfolds alongside agonizing poverty in U.S. society. According to the U.S. Census Bureau, the average poverty threshold for a family of four in 2003 was $18,810; for a family of three, $14,680; for a family of two, $12,015; and for an individual, $9,393.[21] It does not take a great deal of imagination to understand that trying to support oneself or a family on this level of income is a recipe for misery. For instance, the 12.9 million children who grow up poor in the United States are at a heightened risk of stunted physical and intellectual development, less education, and ultimately lower wages in the job market. A study by the Children's Defense Fund, *Defining Poverty and Why It Matters for Children*, notes that each year millions of children who grow up poor will cost society the equivalent of $130 billion of lost contributions to the economy, translated into lower educational achievement and decreased economic productivity. Interestingly, sixty billion dollars were found to start a "regime change" war in Iraq, and tens of billions were appropriated for reconstruction, but monies to launch comprehensive programs to eliminate child poverty are hard to appropriate.[22]

I teach in Dallas at the Perkins School of Theology at Southern Methodist University, which is located in an extremely affluent neighborhood. There are many spacious homes in the neighborhood surrounding the university, with Latino gardeners and maids from the other side of town visibly at work. Unlike poor inner-city areas, the Highland Park community does not count homicide among the leading causes of death for young males, and there are no grim reports of drive-by shootings. Young people growing up in Highland Park are more likely to go to college than drop out of school. If you go for a walk in this neighborhood, you can hardly imagine what it is like owning a home that lacks safe drinking water, yet in places not far from the university along the Texas-Mexico border, about 800,000 poor Latinos who live in so-called colonias lack basic water, electricity, sewer systems, paved roads, and safe and sanitary housing.[23]

I once heard a story from a gardener who works in Highland Park about a three-year-old boy who lived in a colonia. After being missing for three days, the child was found dead at the bottom of a latrine. The relatives and friends who searched for the missing child had looked in the latrine and seen the soles of two shoes belonging to the child in the pit, but they had assumed the little boy had thrown his shoes in the waste well. The colonia lacked a playground, and the little boy had used the outhouse to play on this one occasion. Frustrated, the neighborhood search party returned to the outhouse where the bottom of the boy's shoes could be seen. Horrified, they examined the pit more closely, only to find the child's body buried headfirst in the human waste. He had fallen into the pit.

According to the U.S. Department of Housing and Urban Development, colonia residents have an average income of five thousand dollars a year, and these mostly Latino residents struggle with problems typically associated with developing countries.[24] Poverty means living with a lack of money, decent jobs, adequate schools, housing, health care, and the necessities required for even a minimal version of the American dream. For the boy in the colonia poverty was death, which makes one think about the social location of the church among those who die before their time (Mark 14:7). The prevailing culture teaches us to be suspicious of the poor, who apparently are lazy and don't play by the rules, but Scripture speaks to us of a God who takes their side and initiates a broad-based campaign for social justice in their defense. Hence, we should examine our attitudes about poverty and the labels placed on the poor to better respond to the God who raises prophets who say, "What do you mean by crushing my people, by grinding the face of the poor?" (Isa. 3:15).

The face of global poverty reveals that about half of the world, or nearly three billion people, lives on less than two dollars a day.[25] A close look at the structure of global poverty reveals that the richest 50 million people in Europe and North America have the equivalent income of 2.7 billion people; put differently, 1 percent of the global population takes the same size of cake as the poorest 57 percent.[26] If the prophetic imagination is concerned to criticize situations of socially structured injustice, what good news is proclaimed in a world where the combined wealth of the world's 200 richest people at the end of the 1990s hit $1 trillion and that of 582 million people across the forty-three least developed nations was $146 billion?[27] Although economies in developed nations are supposedly growing, their growth does not match increases in global poverty and rises in desperate conditions of life.

In 2001, there were 497 billionaires in the world holding a combined wealth of $1.54 trillion, which represents more than the combined gross national products of all the nations of sub-Saharan Africa ($929.3 billion) or those of the oil-rich regions of the Middle East and North Africa ($1.34 trillion), or more than the combined incomes of the poorest half of humanity.[28] The Galilean Savior who reveals God's outrage with the scandal of poverty expects the church to be an instrument of good news that advocates living wage laws, access to health care, education, and job training, and a rethinking of the market fundamentalism that does not place moral value or human need above that of money making.[29] Today the words of Gandhi ring truer than ever: "Poverty is the worst form of violence."

Of course, in American history the poor have not been favorably represented in cultural discourse, nor have they been seen to hold values in line with mainstream society. Mostly the poor are treated with suspicion, and the labels attached to them justify social indifference. The social sciences have contributed a great deal to picturing the poor as people who come from unstable families, seek escape from social problems through sexual pleasure and hostility, lack the will to attack the sources of their poverty, are deficient in abstract thinking skills, exhibit low self-esteem, and do not engage in long-term planning.[30] Journalists aware of this academic reading of the poor have reinforced through their writing this negative interpretation of the poor in the popular mind.[31]

In the early 1960s the poor were rediscovered by the publication of Michael Harrington's *The Other America*. This book had been widely read before it influenced the Kennedy administration to address rural poverty. Harrington courageously reminded readers that the prosperity of American society was fundamentally called into question by the forty to fifty million forgotten Americans constituting the ranks of the poor who lived below a minimal standard of decency. Harrington was especially concerned with the invisibility of the poor, who could not be seen by those enjoying the benefits of prosperity, unless the "blinded by affluence"[32] made a great intellectual effort to get off the beaten track.[33]

Government officials had their conscience awakened by Harrington's work. But the poverty of people of color was not yet rendered fully visible by Harrington's contribution—there was yet another America! It took the civil rights movement and urban riots to help refocus poverty, especially on the situation of impoverished African Americans. In a commencement speech delivered at Howard University on June 4, 1965, President Johnson remarked that the "great majority of Negro Americans—the poor, unemployed, and the dispossessed—are another nation. Despite the court orders and the laws, despite the legislative victories and the speeches, for them the walls are rising and the gulf is widening."[34] The nation had become more aware of the grinding poverty of black and white Americans, but Latinos and Native Americans were still largely invisible in poverty debates.

In the 1960s, social scientific theorists who represented the American poor as largely passive and politically disengaged were challenged by race-based economic justice and civil rights struggles in the United States and contradicted by the global poor who mobilized to overcome dependency.[35] In other words, all around the world and within the United States at the time, the people who were, as Martin Luther King Jr. remarked, the people "living in the basement of the Great Society," disputed the conventional view of them, which denied their capacity to use social capital[36] to demand needed economic justice and political change. Nonetheless, America's thinking about the poor—no doubt with the mid-1960s race riots in mind—preferred largely to equate this group with troublemaking and bad values.

In the 1970s, feminists deepened their discussion of women's inequality by discovering working-class women and women of color. They talked of the feminization of poverty, demonstrating through research that women bear a greater burden of poverty in society than men, especially divorced women and single mothers lacking the skills and opportunities for economic achievement. As feminists refocused poverty on the situation of women and children, the vice president of the United States, Spiro Agnew, proposed that one great solution to the problem of poverty was to separate such undeserving people in newly built rural towns.[37] Surely the one out of five children and about half of single mothers in America who live in desperate poverty today represent a protest against the unthinking habits of the better-off that want to keep the poor out of mind.[38]

In the 1980s, when Ronald Reagan came to power, the plight of the poor drew new attention with the popular use of a new label: the underclass. This label was a far better reflection of the hostility of the better-off toward the underside of American society than it was shorthand for compassionately describing the wretched condition of poverty.[39] Herbert Gans warned that the underclass label was exclusionary and that it made it easier for the nonpoor to remain socially distant; moreover, as a code term for the black and Latino poor, it served to hide antiblack and anti-Latino racial antagonism, along with conveniently making the white poor invisible.[40] Although the problems tied to poverty are linked to the economic system and class barriers, use of the underclass label impeded public debate on poverty and fueled the blaming of the poor for their condition.

The American nonpoor rarely confront "the inability of the economy to create enough jobs, especially for unskilled people," says Gans. "It is easier [for them] to believe welfare recipients and, since the mid-1990s, immigrants to be a serious drain on the federal budget than to think about the Pentagon's still-massive drain on the budget."[41] Today the popular press's stress on the underclass, made up mainly of urbanized people of color, reinforces the idea that the poor live by values contrary to those of mainstream society. In short, to the extent that the underclass label is used today to discuss the poor, it erroneously suggests that poverty is the product of mostly individual pathology, which makes the poor unlike better-off Americans.[42]

The poor in America are turned into despised outsiders or distanced from the better-off by statements that include constructions like "those people."[43] We simply avoid understanding poverty by engaging in hard thinking about the massive economic shifts and political decisions that cause the misery of the excluded. The prophetic imagination should serve to remind us that poverty is the product of political and economic realities. In affluent America, where the people in mainline churches are evangelized by Christ to be attentive to the needs of the weak, religious practices should not avoid confronting political decisions, economic structures, and cultural values that determine the life of the marginalized. As Isaiah 58:6–7 observes:

> Is not this the fast that I choose:
>   to loose the bonds of injustice,
>   to undo the thongs of the yoke,
> to let the oppressed go free,
>   and to break every yoke?
> Is it not to share your bread with the hungry,
>   and bring the homeless poor into your house;
> when you see the naked, to cover them,
>   and not to hide yourself from your own kin?

ANNOUNCE GOD'S REIGN

Both the Old and New Testaments condemn poverty, which is especially rooted in a possessive will and destructive power. The Old Testament speaks of the poor using the term *rash*, which refers to people who lack money. The poor are also the *ebyon*, or the person who is marginalized, dependent, and forced to plead for daily bread. The term *ani* may easily be applied to the structure of poverty today, for it refers to those who are humiliated, oppressed, bent over, unjustly exploited, and kept poor. The *anaw* are persons who in their poverty trust in God and God's justice; this term is especially found in the Psalms and the Prophets. In the New Testament, the indigent, wretched, and starving are termed *ptokos*.[44] In short, the situation of people bent over and living in wretchedness is offensive to God.

According to Paul, Jesus "was rich, yet for [our] sakes he became poor, so that by his poverty [we] might become rich" (2 Cor. 8:9). As a missionary, Paul established Christian communities in cities of mixed languages, cultures, and races. He did not apologize for bearing witness to God, who became poor in the crucified One. For Paul, Christ lived in solidarity with people whose economic conditions kept them barely alive. The theological awareness that God seeks life for those who most know economic hardship and despair surrounds the birth of Jesus, which signals a new time:

> [God] has scattered the proud in the thoughts of their hearts,
> He has brought down the powerful from their thrones,
>   and lifted up the lowly;
> he has filled the hungry with good things,
>   and sent the rich away empty. (Luke 1:51b–53)

In other words, Jesus the first evangelist reveals the good news of God's reign among those whose most basic rights are violated by the social order.

Jesus' ministry repeatedly critiqued the false security of the status quo that piously rejected outcasts (Luke 10:25–37) and dared not place the needs of the sick above the law (Mark 2:23; 3:6). In a divided world where historical misery is the by-product of the exploitation and oppression of some human beings by others, Jesus says that acts of justice to benefit the widow, orphan, thirsty, hungry, imprisoned, strangers, and suffering embody God's promise of life in history (Matt. 25:31–46). The followers of Jesus are to place themselves in solidarity with the life and cause of those in most need and show their knowledge of God by acting compassionately. In Jesus Christ, God graciously enters into a saving relationship with human beings, but God's grace draws near in the good news preached to the poor (Matt. 11:5; Luke 4:18) and the promised reign that belongs to them (Luke 6:20).[45]

In our affluent society, we seldom talk about the experience of the early church when Jesus' followers who proclaimed good news in solidarity with the marginalized were subjected to torture, unjustly sentenced, and mistreated by people who believed themselves to be serving God (Mark 13:9–11; Luke 6:22; John 16:1–4).[46] For the early Christian community, the new age started by Jesus Christ also included a discipleship that paid attention to the needs of the poor and that advocated solidarity with those thought unworthy of love (see Acts 3:44–45; 4:24; 11:29–30; Gal. 2:10). Mostly, mainline congregations often put off proclaiming Jesus' identity as a poor Palestinian Jew who reveals the will of God from the edges of society. One afternoon a member of a poor church in Washington, DC who was quite aware of the Word made flesh at the margins and of the humble beginning of the church, said to me, "Jesus is so identified with the poor, his life and way of the cross, his experience with abandonment, his identification with the suffering of the poor, his living the death of the poor. In all this there is a great hope in the church that says things will change."

Today evangelists must necessarily pay attention to the One who teaches us to embody a new way of thinking and acting that is capable of transforming human reality. In part, this requires pondering the theological idea that "a God separated from the poor can be anything except the God who has been revealed to us."[47] In other words, God reveals the world and the historical future of humanity through Christ's presence in the poor. If the reign of God is life in abundance and the positive goal of the mainline church is to work for it, then people need to have their hopes and prophetic imagination stirred up to the point that they engage in an evangelization that rejects a faith witness that turns away from the poor and discredits every effort by them to create peace with justice in the world. Indeed, they will remember that the witness of the church begins with those on the margins of society.

Jesus demonstrated God's saving will in the here and now of his own time. In one story, Jesus is surrounded by people in a simple home in Capernaum with no porch and with a roof anyone who so desired could penetrate to enter. There are few middle-class Christians today who would venture to a simple shack carrying a paralyzed friend for an encounter with a poor man who is said to be a carrier of life and performer of miracles, yet something like this is precisely what took place in Capernaum. Four friends carried a humble stretcher with a silent paralytic on it hoping against hope to find a miracle in a poor neighborhood.[48] In short, a sick person is brought to Jesus the healer by people with the courage to be with the poor. In Capernaum Jesus not only binds the wounds of a poor young man, but he attacks the cultural rules that ensure his oppression.[49]

The healing of the paralytic by Jesus anticipates the turn to the voiceless and excluded other that concerns theologians and ethicists in our day.[50] In the story, the reality of God was manifested in the suffering of the paralytic, whose healing interrupted the authority and experience of theological elites. Jesus' opponents were scandalized by what took place, and they accused him of blasphemy or placing himself on the same level with God (cf. John 10:33). But in Capernaum that day, in the life of an apparently helpless human being, God entered history with empowering hope and liberating grace. The elite who accused Jesus of blasphemy come off like some present-day Christians who believe faith and the demands of love for the suffering are opposing realities, yet in Capernaum the God who disrupts the history made by dominant groups draws us to the side of a devalued human being. God is on the underside of history!

The story of the healed paralytic evangelizes us by suggesting that the act of following Jesus gives rise to authentic love for the people at the edges of society. We see this in the action of the four friends who followed Jesus by doing something for a person defined by public piety or the established ideology as a nonperson. The kingdom of God was present in Jesus' healing and pardoning activity in Capernaum; indeed, Mark tells us that the reign of God drew near when Jesus announced the forgiveness of sins without insisting on repentance or amends. If the standard theological wisdom of the mainline religious authorities said the paralytic was merely an outcast and hopeless sinner, Jesus' forgiveness delivers the paralytic into the kingdom of God and heals his real misery by restoring life! In other words, representing the reign of God in the world requires a radical social practice that rejects a conventional piety that aligns itself with an alienating social order.

I can imagine that some who gathered around Jesus in Capernaum shared with others how "Jesus went about all the cities and villages, teaching in their synagogues, and proclaiming the good news of the kingdom, and curing every disease and every sickness" (Matt. 9:35). People who suffered need, were sick, imprisoned, homeless, landless, jobless, weighed down by unimaginable burdens, wept as a consequence of real oppression, or longed to trust in God became amazingly aware that "God's gifts of salvation bear witness to the presence of the deliverer."[51] In Capernaum, the people who gathered around Jesus were amazed by all they witnessed, especially when he told the paralytic, "Stand up, take your mat, and go to your home" (Mark 2:10). No reader of the Gospel of Mark can be unaware that the paralytic's tears must have certainly turned to laughter (see Luke 6:21) once he experienced God's redeeming love.

In the twenty-first century, mainline churches are pressed to discern what it means to be Christian in a crucified world. There is another story that shows Jesus engaged in table talk at the home of Simon the Pharisee that helps clarify the meaning of the community of discipleship and prophetic evangelism. On this occasion, Jesus is on friendly terms with a Pharisee who represents traditional piety in the story. In Capernaum Jesus was with a wretched human being; now we find him with someone of social status. At some point in the course of the dinner a prostitute joins the party, and she shows Jesus extraordinary gratitude.[52] Luke reports an incredible scene in which the woman washes Jesus' feet with her tears, wipes them with her hair, kisses his feet, and anoints Jesus with ointment from an alabaster flask (Luke 7:36–50).

Who really experiences God's forgiving grace? According to the Gospel of Luke, the sexually exploited prostitute who displays grateful love is nearer to God than Simon. The proper guests are scandalized that Jesus would allow himself to be touched and contaminated by a streetwalker whom they considered beyond redemption; indeed, this may have given them a reason to disassociate Jesus from the line of the prophets. Simon utters the thought, "If this man were a prophet, he would have known who and what kind of woman this is who is touching him—that she is a sinner" (Luke 7:39). But Jesus had no trouble relating to social outcasts, and he refuses here to accept the traditional sanction against the woman. Jesus rejects the vertical discriminations of dominant society and affirms the dignity and worth of the woman who came in off the street. He refused to see her status as below that of anyone at the dinner party.

The mainline religious crowd at the dinner party, believing themselves more virtuous than the prostitute, wanted to keep her voiceless. They could not see her as a person who was overcoming the oppression of the flesh trade by manifesting through her altered life the reign of God. Unlike Simon, who provided Jesus with space in his home at a dinner party, the impure and anguished sex worker unreservedly opened her heart to God's ultimate love present in Christ. Simon's negative judgment of the woman reflects a conventional understanding that saw harlots as figures of low repute (Gen. 34:31; Judg. 11:1; 1 Kgs. 22:38; Isa. 1:21; Jer. 3:3; Ezek. 16:30); indeed, harlots were ostracized and could even be punished by death (Gen. 38:24; Lev. 21:9).[53] Perhaps a male dinner guest invited the woman, especially since men could enjoy a harlot's service with no legal penalties (Gen. 38:15ff.).

Although the text does not give any indication of this kind of conversation, I can imagine Jesus, before telling the story of the two debtors, revealing that the prostitute Rahab (Josh. 2:1–21) and three other women who were involved in sex scandals are related to him—Tamar, Ruth, and Bathsheba. I can imagine that Simon, who did not see the woman as a daughter of God, was likely shocked least by the sex scandals associated with these relatives of Jesus and more shocked by the biographical detail that only Bathsheba among these four relatives was Jewish. Whatever sidebar conversation took place at dinner, Simon's criticism is countered by Jesus with the story of the two debtors, which illustrates the reality of God and God's grace active in the response of a humiliated and oppressed prostitute.

Jesus explains why he allowed a despised woman to touch him. The little parable about two debtors presents us with two forgiven people. Interestingly, the contrast in the parable is not that between a person who is forgiven and another who is not; instead, opposites are imaged by great debt and little debt, profound thankfulness and hardly a word of gratitude.[54] The parable instructs the Pharisee and the guests representing mainline piety and social privilege that in the new age of Christ they should not despise the poverty-stricken or rejected, who are loved by God. Moreover, those who feel content in their high social status and cosmetic religious piety should not take their redemption for granted but be thankful for God's love and forgiveness.[55]

This story of the dinner party directs the attention of mainline theologians and believers to despised outcasts.[56] Jesus challenged people who had a high opinion of their theological view with the God of the poverty-stricken, the scandalous, the helpless, the despised, and the hopeless. The prostitute who showed a great love for Jesus knew what the self-righteous dinner guests failed to recognize: God called her into a future where "all tears are wiped away" (Isa. 25:8; Rev. 7:17; 21:4). She was filled with that prophetic imagination that hopes for the coming future of God in this life. As one of the despised of the earth, the gospel empowered hope and human dignity in her. Like the paralytic in Capernaum, she could stand on her own feet and claim her voice. She became a conscious subject of the reign of God aware of her dignity before God. In short, the healed paralytic and the loved prostitute embodied the good news of God aware that they now "can get up out of the dust and help themselves."[57]

CONCLUSION

Mainline churches have been rightly concerned to revitalize their congregational lives, but the focus on church growth pays too little attention to the importance of understanding the gospel in the world of the crucified poor. The recovery of the logic of evangelism at the core of church mission cannot remain captive to the proclamation of a "user friendly gospel." Instead, as the church bears witness to the message of Christ it will find its identity in the world beyond plans for numerical growth or mere reference to the private affairs of humankind. As mainline churches seek to communicate the good news of Christ relevantly and critically aided by a prophetic imagination, they will criticize their culturally captive Christianity as well as the life-denying structures of society from the perspective of poor and racially rejected people.

In American mainline religious circles the poor are labeled in morally negative terms, which allows them to be kept at a social distance from the nonpoor. The prophetic imagination empowers members of mainline churches who are not poor to discover Christ in disinherited people who are sick, crippled, homeless, and who are prostitutes, debtors, and beggars on the urban streets and rural roads (Luke 14:21–23; Matt. 11:2–5; 18:23–35). The good news of Jesus offers dehumanized persons a new life-altering reality. Mainline churches that seek to continue the mission of Jesus will proclaim a gospel that drives out of society the structures that create poverty and brokenness.

Mainline Christians who read their Scriptures from the perspective of rejected people will not be surprised to discover in the written accounts of faith that the poor and racially despised are often instruments of God's self-disclosure. Mainline churches engaged in evangelism need to question whether or not their witness recognizes Christ in mission at the margins of society. In the same way that Jesus in Simon's house and with the young paralytic questioned the purity system, the church is called to evangelize the world in light of the alternative consciousness and vision of God's favorable time in Christ (Luke 4:18–19). In conclusion, the prophetic imagination tells us that in a world where people die prematurely for the benefit of the nonpoor, the alternative vision of the gospel begs to be proclaimed and prophetically enacted.

GAMES

I saw children playing
on the corner wearing
smiles that old prayers

often bid for the whole
block. abuelitas came
out of tired buildings

to sit on stoops tying
unlaced sneakers with
wrinkled hands made

before time. they looked
up smiling at the old
man with stories that

cough up on all the
corners loud enough
to raise blinds and

open eyes in all the
windows. kids who
think games never

end made the street
sing a babble of
fun that left imprints

on the crowds on the
well-kept sidewalks.
we drew nearer to the

truth that sabado
afternoon simply
to drink it still.

3

They Go to the Altar

It was not difficult growing up in the South Bronx in a community dominated by chronic poverty and street violence to realize that evangelism was not an abstract idea but a way to live in the awareness that the reign of God proclaimed by Christ offers life for those surrounded by death-dealing conditions. My mother's shrine of Catholic saints sitting atop a dresser in her bedroom reinforced the belief that answers to daily problems were to be worked out in the realm of everyday existence in light of the enduring presence of God in our lives. When she lit candles to San Martín de Porres requesting release from poverty, her religious behavior strongly spoke of a deep faith in a God of love who hears the cry of voiceless people.

In our overcrowded, single-bedroom apartment, the reign of God was not known in abstract theological discourse or in light of the interpretations of church traditions and texts made by celebrated theologians. Instead, from a Puerto Rican woman who never finished grade school I learned that the gospel is to be taken seriously in contexts of poverty and injustice that demand social change. Today I realize that this woman who prayed every evening at her bedroom altar was one of the abandoned and plundered of the world, a member of that mass of humanity living on the edge of death. In spite of living in constant poverty, she kept going back to the altar to find hope in God's promise of new life. Women like her who live in the barrio tell us evangelism should surrender to the will of God present in the expectation of those suffering social rejection and economic hardship.

The barrio is the other America that does not participate in modern society's idolization of science, technology, and wealth. Instead, the single mothers you find there who light candles at home, engage in daily devotions, and attend worship at storefront churches place their ultimate trust in the God who freely sides with the powerless and is never unresponsive like idols (Ps. 115). Long before postmodern discourse was intellectually fashionable, these marginal women of the barrio predicted things would fall apart by questioning the belief that America is God's global herald, by incarnating the injustices of the capitalist market system in their own lives, and by rejecting the alleged superior wisdom of mainstream and Eurocentric Christianity.

I believe mainline Christians can renew their understanding of evangelism by relating to barrio people who know the message of Jesus is good news because it brings life in the face of death-dealing forces and racist ideologies. Nonetheless, not many mainline Christians turn to the barrio or inner city to find theological insight for their churches' evangelizing activities. They seem to prefer the security of their ecclesial settings, where they gather to nourish church growth dreams while remembering the words of great religious leaders such as Archbishop Oscar Romero, Martin Luther King Jr., Howard Thurman, Dietrich Bonhoeffer, Mother Teresa, and Thomas Merton. These memorable Christians have deeply enriched the life of the church, yet people of the barrio who have cultivated a great intimacy with God also offer mainline Christians theological insight for seeing the Word made flesh in the struggle for life.

Barrio Christians remind mainline church members to imagine the renewal of society by deeply considering the words of Isaiah 1:16–17, "Wash yourselves; make yourselves clean; remove the evil of your doings from before my eyes; cease to do evil, learn to do good; seek justice, rescue the oppressed; defend the orphan, plead for the widow." Barrio Christians open up new meanings of the gospel for the mainline church when they interpret Scripture and confess that God lived among us (John 1:14) like an abused person (Phil. 2:7). Barrio evangelism enthusiastically defines the context of God in marginality, especially acknowledging that God first loves those whose life is systemically crushed each day. The barrio evangelizes the mainline church to the extent that its members are open to its alternative perception of reality and faith. As one refugee from El Salvador remarked to me in 2002:

> The evangelism that does not give itself to the basic needs of human existence or is indifferent to injustice, repression, human abuse, exploitation and to discrimination and racism is not committed to God's project of life. The system of life in the United States is a system that makes you blind and confused. We need to talk about a spirituality of life, of defending the poor, the exploited and the humiliated, of desiring to make straight the ways of justice.

Believing in the biblical God as taught by Jesus means crying out in the barrio with the psalmist, "The LORD is a stronghold for the oppressed, a stronghold in times of trouble. And those who know your name put their trust in you, for you, O LORD, have not forsaken those who seek you" (Ps. 9:9–10). The alternative perception of reality mainline Christians encounter in the barrio includes Latinos expressing thanks for the grace that led people across the sea, the Rio Grande, and through the desert to a new land (Exod. 3:17). In prayer services, grandmothers praise God with Psalm 9, reflecting on the prayer's openness to the cries of the humiliated and trampled. They recognize the world is still filled with the injustice the psalmist addresses insofar as the innocent are abused, the poor are oppressed, and people live in fear. However, *abuelas* (grandmothers) never tire of shouting, "Rise up, O LORD! Do not let mortals prevail; let the nations be judged before you" (Ps. 9:19).

In the barrio, proclaiming the good news recognizes that human beings degrade themselves when they fail to have their compassion aroused by a hurt neighbor. In this faith witness, the role of the innocent bystander who observes injustices suffered by others and does nothing is rejected. Barrio evangelism declares God's blessing comes when people serve Jesus by feeding the hungry, satisfying the thirsty, visiting the sick, welcoming the stranger, clothing the naked, going to the imprisoned, and offering more life to those denied it. Latino Christians announcing the good news assume service to the least of God's people leads away from self-absorption and toward a genuine discipleship that shows the nearness of the reign of God. One theologian has described this kind of spirituality in this way:

> It involves not withdrawal but engagement; not shutting one's eyes to evil but opening one's eyes clearly to see both the individual and systemic reasons for that evil; not emptying the mind so that the Spirit can flood into the emptiness, but filling the mind with statistics about who doesn't eat and why not, about where concentrations of wealth (and consequent injustices) are located, about indignities suffered by powerless people.[1]

Barrio Christians use the gospel both to individually evangelize others and to discern the work of God in local contexts. I will never forget the day Julia came to church with an urgent need to give testimony and burning with a spirituality of engagement that had matured in El Salvador, where Christians sacrificed their lives defending the rights of the poor. She was on her way to work one early morning at a large tourist hotel in Washington, DC, where she cleaned guest rooms for a living. As she walked toward the Metro station, she noticed a young family outside of her apartment complex sitting on the sidewalk with all their worldly possessions scattered about the dirty street. The sight of a young family apparently homeless and feeling utterly abandoned reminded Julia that Jesus, who knew the agony of being a refugee when just a child, said, "Blessed are you who are poor, for yours is the kingdom of God" (Luke 6:20).

Julia always talked about being evangelized by the faith witness of Salvadoran archbishop Oscar Romero, who believed the poor who endured the ongoing crucifixion of Jesus in history would see a new world in history. In Sunday worship, Julia simply wanted to testify that nothing defined the church more clearly than accompanying those with no space to be human beings. Her early morning meeting with a homeless family was nothing less than an encounter with the Christ who draws us to God in unexpected ways. Julia shared that all she wanted to do that morning was act in fidelity to the gospel without giving a thought to what this could mean to her own situation. Her ultimate concern was to embrace the problems of a young family then on a suburban sidewalk with no place to turn.

The Scripture text that came to Julia that morning while walking toward the couple was Jeremiah 22:13: "Woe to him who builds his house by unrighteousness, and his upper rooms by injustice; who makes his neighbors work for nothing, and does not give them their wages." Julia saw in the homeless family Christ, who called her to practice justice and not shut her eyes to the cause of a poor family. Nothing could prevent Julia that morning from approaching the family on the street with the love that demonstrates commitment to the God who exalts those of low degree. What became clear to me from Julia's testimony was that it was not an intensely privatized form of faith seeking to withdraw from the world; instead, her faith witness pointed to the importance of living out God's will in relationship to others and by discovering Jesus in brokenness (Luke 24:35).[2]

Julia knew nothing of following a Jesus who says to turn away from the world; rather, the root of her spirituality was the experience of confronting a system of life that crushes people. She approached the young family bearing witness to a gospel that offers justice and compassion for neighbors. She learned the family had been forcibly evicted from a studio apartment for not paying two months' back rent. Because she understood that following Christ meant going out of her way to respond to the needs of others, Julia invited the young family to live with her until they could find work and an apartment. She found God not with the landlord who evicted the young family, but by opening her heart to the young couple and helping them find work, housing, and healthcare for their baby. She even called a friend who managed a laundromat to send a pickup truck to help collect the things scattered about the street and store them.

Julia provided the young family with shelter for a couple of months. She explained how "things worked" in the States to them and linked Rafael with social networks to help him find work. She responded to the reality of a beaten-down family by doing what was necessary to help them get back on their feet (Pss. 10:15–18; 68:5–10). Her simple act of justice did not tear down the social system that exploits the poor and disposes of them when their labor is no longer needed, but she modeled what it means to be faithful day by day to God's reign on the individual level in a world of injustices. Julia perfected her love for God by acting in a way that bore witness in the world to the future God promises to human beings. Today Rafael's family has an apartment and Rafael has a good-paying job that enables his wife to care for their baby. Because they were evangelized by a simple act of caring, they remember Christ who approached them in a neighbor.

Today many members of the dominant culture look away from the barrio for new ways to view the sacred, especially given that an unfolding "spiritual quest" culture continues to captivate the interest of mainline Christians.[3] Religious interests are no longer limited to the discourse of theologians and clergy in American society, which raises the question of whether or not the Christian heritage is losing value in the spiritual search of ordinary people. Persons integrated into the frame of reference produced by a largely white, middle-class culture are now more likely to engage in self-directed spiritual quests beyond the boundaries of organized religious life than they are concerned to find Jesus at the center of the reality of poor barrio communities.[4]

Of course, there are church leaders seeking to live out their faith in relationship to the living Christ who are ill-at-ease with our society's emerging "cafeteria spirituality," which encourages people to pick and choose religious frames of reference from a spiritual marketplace. They correctly wonder whether or not the future promises further membership decline as Americans adopt multiple religious traditions and fashions them into a singular religious worldview. Let us look a bit more closely below at the new spiritual quest culture.[5]

SPIRITUAL QUEST CULTURE

The great myth of modern society was that scientific rationality was supposed to replace superstitious religious worldviews. In fact, religious beliefs and practices have not been driven out of modern life; rather, they have increased and established new and various realignments with culture. Sociologists tell us that in the past fifty years in the United States, religious beliefs and practices have reflected individual concern to reevaluate the meaning of the sacred.[6] Because too many churches seem unable to meet the religious needs of people, American culture reflects a desire on the part of many to experientially deepen spirituality by visiting New Age bookshops, inventing new languages of faith, or picking up clues about spiritual life in films, television, and the virtual world.[7] In other words, spirituality for many Americans today is not limited to any one place or strict adherence to a singular religious tradition.

In *After Heaven: Spirituality in America since the 1950s*, sociologist Robert Wuthnow claims that profound changes in American religious practices have unfolded in post–World War II society. Wuthnow examines changes in American religiosity by reflecting on data collected from two hundred individuals representing Christian fundamentalism, Christian denominational groups, Eastern religions, Native American spirituality, New Age spirituality, and twelve-step programs. He argues that the central metaphor for American spiritual life has shifted from a "dwelling spirituality" where God inhabits a definite place in the universe and creates a sacred place for humans (the family, church, home, and nation) to a "seeker spirituality" in which "individuals search for sacred moments that reinforce their conviction that the divine exists" (based on self-direction and momentary glimpses of the sacred).[8]

In the 1940s and 1950s, Americans knew God best in their congregations and family life. This dwelling spirituality was a kind of "formulaic religiosity, a faith in faith itself, a simple affirmation in the existence of God, a belief that all would be well if one worked hard."[9] Dwelling spirituality withdrew Americans into a spiritual fortress where even the horrors of the Jewish Holocaust and a racially divided America could be denied.[10] In time, the experience of wars, genocide, the murder of political figures, civil strife, distrust of organized religion, and material wealth issued forth in a reevaluation of the sacred. Moreover, as the postwar years brought geographical, occupational, and economic mobility; higher levels of education; institutional transformations; and suburbanization, Americans left aside the dwelling spirituality of the 1940s and 1950s. In other words, "faith was no longer something people inherit but something for which they strive."[11]

The seeker spirituality that issued forth in the 1960s and 1970s encouraged a questioning of the standard ways to understand who God is and where God can be found. Influenced by the racial justice movement, the antiwar movement, and the countercultural movement, many Americans opposed the spirituality of respectable houses of worship and white definitions of God. This new orientation to the sacred meant that more Americans pursued religiosity open to a complex variety of human experiences. In fact, spiritual inspiration was found in "the struggles of the poor, from the rich spiritual traditions of African Americans, from other world religions, from rock music and contemporary art, and from changing understandings of gender and sexuality."[12] Zen, Yoga, retreats, twelve-step programs, and the mysteries of nature helped persons explore religious experience. Thus, this seeker spirituality encouraged individuals to step out of their familiar spaces.[13]

By the 1980s the optimism in the perfectibility of humanity and the power of scientific rationality to solve all problems was declining, while individuals sought more public space in which to produce meaningful existence.[14] At this time, born-again Christians became engaged in politics, with distinct views on sexual lifestyle, the communist threat, the war on drugs, the welfare state, abortion, and capitalism.[15] The basic spiritual agenda of born-again Christians was to inspire conservative social change in American society.[16] Using spiritual discipline and Bible-based beliefs to claim public space, televangelists such as Jerry Falwell and Pat Robertson took advantage of American feelings of spiritual restlessness by "reasserting so-called traditional values, including closeness to God and a disciplined respect for moral authority."[17] Nonetheless, born-again Christian spirituality was not popularly embraced because it could not cater to most American seekers.[18]

Although sociological research shows fundamentalists did not seriously change the way Americans viewed God, in the 1980s born-again Christian political activism dominated media perceptions of what it meant to be Christian and American. The political alliances forged that involved groups such as the Moral Majority and the 700 Club helped to deafen spiritual seekers and the liberal press to the words of persecuted classes in Central America and dehumanized persons of color in the United States. In time, the 50 million born-again Christians set up 450 colleges, 18,000 schools, 275 periodicals, 70 evangelical publishing houses, and 3300 Christian bookshops, which had no small social impact.[19] Whether or not born-again Christians changed American minds about God was least worrisome than asking, How did this largely white, middle-class, conservative Protestant movement influence political attitudes and behavior?

Wade Clark Roof notes that "the spiritual implies the transforming presence of the sacred, a presence made real, indeed created, through the persuasive power of narrative and symbol."[20] Jerry Falwell and Pat Robertson used Christian narrative and biblical symbols to make themselves visible in the Republican party and to promote their views on the sacred with lasting influence on American political values and practices.[21] As conservative vocal elites, their spiritual message did not focus on economic, racial, gender, and international inequalities; rather, their language of American superiority inspired divisions in public culture between conservatives and progressive groups, reinforced attitudes about extending the international boundaries of American capitalist domination in the world, and inspired public policy reactions about the browning of America.

Seeker spirituality indicates that Americans yearn to have direct contact with something greater than themselves, their politics, and their cultural experiences. The American need for contact with the sacred is reflected in the fascination with angels, consumption of religious books, the increased examination of religious themes in talk shows, film, MTV, and musical forms such as country music, hip-hop, reggae, rap, and salsa.[22] Some believe seeker spirituality reflects a time of transition in America to increased moral relativism, a disuniting multiculturalism, a postecclesial and post-Christian reality. Others hold the view that openness to new sources of spirituality and the desire to have new religious experiences signals a renewal of divine awareness in the wider American public and the importance of having a more fluid and less dogmatic approach to religiosity.

I think the shift in American spirituality over the last fifty years verifies the postmodernist idea of the end of the era of authoritative narratives. With the increased recognition of the plurality of voices in American society, individuals are more apt to cast a wide net in the religious marketplace regarding their spiritual practices. Seeker spirituality is all about individuals concerned to find religious meaning in changing, secular, and uncertain environments. Meanwhile, the people living in places like the barrio continue to challenge us to move beyond any purely subjective spiritual agenda. Their oppressive conditions of life challenge the current trend of self-directed religiosity. The ultimate structure of life urges spiritual seekers to stop navel gazing and find a more complete vision of the sacred with outcasts from the dominant culture.

In a positive vein, American religious experience over the last five decades shows that spirituality must continually change and transform itself to be meaningful. Negatively, contemporary mainstream spirituality shows subjective experience is so privileged that it has virtually exclusive legitimacy as a way of knowing the self, others, and ultimate reality.[23] This subjective focus coupled with the individualism of American culture tends to result and reinforce a vertically oriented private spirituality (the individual/God above).[24] Seeker spirituality keeps alive the role of religion in society, but its largely individual and vertically oriented focus encourages persons to approach selected spiritual traditions in ways that omit exploration of their spiritual message in relation to others and in the lives of the oppressed and needy.

BARRIO SPIRITUALITY EVANGELIZES

If American spirituality today frees individuals to seek the sacred in a great variety of religious symbols, stories, images, and diversifying religious behaviors, the time is ripe for persons to take a journey into the barrio, where Latino subgroups assert that living in the spirit of Jesus results in a spirituality that confronts the secularity around us and contextualizes the good news in activity directed toward the reign of God. Barrio spirituality aims to awaken

PRAISE

in this barrio
we long to breathe
God's grace on the

corner where Tito
shot his young uncle
following an argument

about a job at the
local A&P supermarket.
we long to see unshed

tears in the light
that keeps us from
being trampled under

and gives us strength
to count the years. in
this barrio we seek heaven

where there is no
dying a little each
day nor beginning and

end. but today with
the bloodstains fresh
beneath our feet only

images of the people
who eat their fill
while promising better

days to come, arise. so
deaf God we gather and pray
let no more lives be crushed

nor a single child fall and
give us hope to live the
next hour. . . .

persons estranged from the church and individuals confused within it to an existential awareness of the experience of the God of reconciling unity, who asks people not to store up treasures on earth. Spiritual seekers who find religious depth in the barrio learn to confront the world strengthened by Jesus' words: "Take courage; I have conquered the world!" (John 16:33).

Seeker spirituality requires the exercise of constant discernment to prevent confusing the ultimate structure of reality with culture or new patterns of religious behavior. Seeker spirituality lacks a concern for the ethical-political dimensions of religious experience, an understanding of the biblical God of justice, and serious reflection on the ethical aspects of the spiritual traditions selected by an individual for constructing his or her religiousness. Barrio spirituality is informed by the belief in the God of the helpless revealed by Jesus of Nazareth, who says, "I am the LORD your God, who brought you out of the land of Egypt, out of the house of slavery; you shall have no other gods before me" (Exod. 20:2–3). Barrio Christians seek to remain faithful to Jesus, while refusing to make Christian life dependent on prevailing cultural norms.

Barrio Christians offer a helping hand to seekers with their spirituality that responds to the total demand of God through social and personal witness. People in the barrio recognize that behind every form of social injustice is the God who hears the cry of the abused and leads them to new life. The religious experience of the barrio also reflects an intense personal trust in the God who empowers us by calling attention to the social and cultural horrors of the cross in Golgotha, Latin America, the South Bronx, the Rio Grande Valley, and the inner city. Barrio Christians challenge the evils of the dominant culture by calling them into question in the name of God and in light of a prophetic stance. Hence, barrio spirituality speaks to the church's evangelizing impulse by holding up a God of life and avoiding the kind of Christianity that conforms to the status quo.

Mainline Christians about to jump on the seeker wagon and who are open to creative cross-cultural and cross-contextual encounters will find that in the barrio Latinos are focused on faith in Jesus Christ, who refused to disguise reality or encourage religious escapism. Barrio Christians recognize that no trial or distress can separate people within or outside of the barrio from the limitless love of God or the world-shattering presence of Jesus Christ. Barrio spirituality renews the faith witness of the wider church by keeping people close to the good news and asserting that authentic piety situates the gospel among the real sins of society. In the words of Archbishop Romero, "A gospel that doesn't unsettle, a word of God that doesn't get under anyone's skin, a word of God that doesn't touch the real sin of the society in which it is being proclaimed, what gospel is that?"[25]

Christians in the barrio evangelize the church when they declare that God speaks today in a very clear voice through the needs, rights, dignity, culture, gifts, and faith of crucified people. The clear voice of God heard through the barrio enables persons to take a stand against a money-grubbing society and remain faithful to Jesus, who reveals God's love from the cross. Barrio spirituality says Jesus looks favorably on those who find God revealed by the racially despised (Luke 10:25–37), closer to the poor than to the guardians of mainline piety, and with people who act out God's will over those who cry "Lord, Lord." (Luke 10:25; Matt. 7:21–23) and do nothing to change structures of sin in the world. In other words, Jesus is the daily bread that keeps people fully awake, fully alive, and fully aware of God's Word and demands.

I find that the spiritual insight of people in the barrio renews mainline church witness when it proclaims that Jesus gathered his followers in the marginal region of Galilee and had them face the world with a message of justice, love, and hope. It announces that Jesus was present among the sick whom he healed, the hungry he fed, and the rich he converted to the justice of God and service to the poor. Jesus was at home among strangers, the destitute, widows, women, the imprisoned, the rejected, and the downhearted. He visited like any ordinary person in cities, villages, and religious centers to minister to anyone ready to be transformed by the gospel or open to the love of God. Because Jesus went everywhere and avoided no one, barrio spirituality proclaims that he is the ultimate protest against everything in us that refuses to be called "out of darkness into his marvelous light" (1 Pet. 2:9). He teaches us to see the world anew.

Mainline Christianity and seeker spirituality mostly reflect the norms of contemporary society, which makes them unable to critique the dominant social, political, economic, and cultural values. Mainline churches will find it difficult to evangelize individuals and American culture unless they see the alternative understanding of life offered by the gospel of Jesus of Nazareth. Barrio spirituality resists counting how many people are sitting in church pews, the religious endorsement of the American way of life, and the faith shopping that ejects the justice of God from worldly affairs. People in the barrio drawn into hopeful community and nurtured by gospel stories that help them see the world differently are the first to say that evangelism is all about how good God is toward us.

We need new eyes to evangelize others in a broken world. We cannot permit ourselves to see reality through a lens of dividing hostilities, the view that others are strangers and enemies, and the belief that poverty and racial violence are inevitable in life. Latinos see Jesus at work transforming an oppressive society into a spiritual union of human beings that hope in the world to come and struggle for unity in this world now. They know that walking with Jesus means adopting a fresh look at life in society. From among the many stories that speak to us about Jesus tearing down and destabilizing customary worldviews, one story about faith as sight stands out in barrio spirituality—that of the road to Emmaus.

FAITH AS SIGHT

The story of the road to Emmaus invites us to move beyond crushing experiences and notice the God who walks alongside us (Luke 24:13–35). Our attention is drawn to the stranger who walked with the two disciples and guided them toward a more perfect grasp of truth. The plot is simple. Two followers of Jesus walking to a village are overcome with feelings of fear, confusion, and despair while talking about the events of the past week. The teacher who taught them to love the downtrodden, who knew the authorities were out to get him, and who entered Jerusalem to the sound of cheering crowds, departed the city executed on a dumpsite like other lawbreakers. The disciples who witnessed Jesus' crucifixion at the hands of religious and political rulers thought then that those with political, economic, and religious power could stand in the way of God's will for human beings.

The two disciples had grown more fearful than in the days of meeting behind closed doors with Jesus. I can well imagine they talked at length about the chief priests and Roman authorities who got rid of oppositional groups by killing their leaders. Although they believed that God hears the cries of the abused for justice, now the two were unsure that the anguished shouts of their crucified Lord reached beyond this world where crosses are prepared by rulers for those who attempt to change it. Their feelings of abandonment by God and their anxious groping for answers to understand what happened in Jerusalem may well have pushed out of their minds any confidence in Jesus' words of promised good news. But the plot of this story of seeing anew thickens.

A stranger who joins the disciples on their walk asks them what they are discussing. Departing Jerusalem convinced of their interpretation of events, the two disciples do not recognize that the stranger is their Lord. But they do not tell him to get lost. They answer the questions of the uninformed stranger by sharing aspects of the message of Jesus, "a prophet mighty in deed and word before God and all the people" (Luke 24:19). They tell the stranger how powerful religious and political leaders in Jerusalem sentenced Jesus to death. They even share the witness of the women who reported the body was missing from the tomb.

With the stranger, the disciples discover that neither their nationalist hope nor incipient psychological despair is the last word on the action-packed week that had passed; instead, the final word is the love of God on the cross that inspires one to live at the disposition of others and for the sake of goodness in the world. Because they took the time to walk and talk with a stranger, the disciples become aware that "God is yet among human beings despite Good Friday."[26] But their eyes open slowly to the reality of God present in the risen Lord, who shows God's power over sin and abusive worldly power. In spite of walking with the stranger for several hours, the two disciples are still unable to discern that it is the risen Christ with them making the fulfillment of God's love for humanity a living reality in their lives.

The stranger patiently listens to them and finally expresses disapproval of their lack of faith and their disbelief in all that the prophets had spoken (Luke 24:25). He proceeds to talk to them of the Scriptures and to frame their faith in light of the memory of Moses and the prophets. Still, the two disciples show a sluggish theological understanding, and no new way of seeing emerges for them. They cannot yet believe that for Christ death issued forth in life. The witness of the Scriptures, the testimony of women, and the nearness of God on a stony road have not quickly opened their eyes to Christ, the human other that unveils the real meaning of existence. Being evangelized into the reality of God or experiencing a spiritual awakening on the road with a stranger is just not something the disciples expected to have that afternoon.

As they approach the village, the two disciples almost lose the opportunity to deepen their understanding of God as the stranger prepares to leave. If the stranger were allowed to leave, the disciples would have missed seeing the God who knows the suffering of the silenced, the Lord who condemns injustice, cares for the helpless, and shows his wounds. Today this means barrio strangers encountered along the way should not be turned away, since they reveal "the truth of the Emmaus road story that the risen Christ journeys with us whether we know it or not."[27] Luckily the disciples do not miss the opportunity to learn to see the world anew. They strongly urge the stranger to remain with them that night—to break bread together.

The disciples become aware that the risen Jesus is with them at supper when the stranger acts out the story of redemption by breaking bread. Only when they move from talking about the events of the past week to the act of sharing bread with a fellow traveler are they able to see the truth in their confused minds and uncertain hearts. Once the stranger becomes the host at the dinner table and gives the disciples bread to eat their eyes are opened to the Lord among them. They reflect, "'Were not our hearts burning within us while he was talking to us on the road, while he was opening the scriptures to us?'" (Luke 24:32). By showing hospitality to a stranger as Jesus taught them to do, they are afforded a reawakening experience to the living God. The gospel message is clear: God is seen in the practice of breaking bread with strangers.

The good news was something given to the disciples by a stranger in a violent world. The power of God present in the suffering of history made justice,
love, and unity real for travelers that day. The two disciples realized at the dinner table that they were in the presence of the very Lord whom Mary declared
would bring a time when the hungry would be fed and the rich sent away
empty (Luke 1:53). As their eyes opened, they likely remembered the time
Jesus fed a multitude in the desert by using their meager provisions and that
of unnamed yet provision-bearing women (Matt. 14:13–21).[28] Not far from
their minds that night were the poor, blind, hungry, women, sick, and racially
rejected who were invited to a dinner turned down by the better-off (Luke
14:15–24). God's reign has a way of coming in the simple fellowship with
strangers made friends by the breaking of bread together.

The Emmaus story reminds us about what people in the barrio know spir-
itually, namely, that Jesus makes all things new in the context of everyday life.
Jesus calls us in moments that are not so extraordinary to be open to the living God who is present in unfamiliar people who are battered by the sin of the
world. In the Emmaus story, hospitality is a sign of a far deeper spirituality and
more meaningful evangelization, because it compels the disciples to move
away from their own self-centered thoughts to the God who is close to human
suffering and who draws people into God's will by the revelation of Jesus crucified and risen. In other words, the murdered Jesus shared a meal with the
disciples and made them aware that the crucified of history reveal the truth
about reality. The risen One was a sign of a new creation in which God sides
with the crucified to empower the process that brings peace and justice to all.

From the perspective of the barrio, the story of Emmaus says that following the risen Lord means overcoming the reality of crucifixion as a model of
society. It tells us the bread of life will always come to us from the risen victim
who brings the world to the full realization of its being. The story of Emmaus
makes plain that authentic spirituality does not consist of self-pity or in
defending the interests of one's national group. Jesus' act of table fellowship
opened the disciples' eyes to a powerful God of life that wills justice as the final
word on suffering and death. The story of Emmaus reveals the disciples' weak-
nesses as a kind of strength used by Jesus to build community between human
beings in a newly structured vision of life together in the world. With a deepened theological awareness, the disciples moved from sorrow to joy, from self-
pity to announcing good news, and from the lonely road to traveling with
Christ.

People in the barrio believe the Emmaus story tells us the truth of the risen
Lord is not "grounded in whether or not the tomb was empty but in the ongoing experience of Jesus as a living reality, as a figure of the present."[29] This
story is about following Jesus in the present by not accepting things the way

they are and by nurturing eyes that see the world differently and ears that hear the risen Lord speaking through strangers. The Emmaus story suggests that by eagerly valuing the gift of strangers it is possible to encounter a world far richer than ever imagined. Mainline Christians and spiritual seekers can find Jesus by breaking bread with strangers in the barrio who have something to say, whose words about life are different, who declare that God rules over the heart of human beings and brings good news to all historical realities.

CONCLUSION

Today some church leaders attempt to renew local congregations' ranks by removing signs of denominational affiliation from church names in order to appeal to spiritual seekers who are distrustful of organized religion. Mainline church renewal will more significantly result from taking the barrio seriously as a context that offers a fresh interpretation of the basics of faith for spiritual seekers within and outside of the church. Members of mainline denominations whose leadership now ponders whether or not mainline Christianity has a future should then not ignore the opportunity for renewal offered by Christians in the barrio.[30] The misunderstood and ignored people of the barrio are eager to evangelize the mainline church with a spirituality that holds that one becomes a human being by befriending strangers, by embodying community, and by demonstrating God's reconciling purpose for the world.

Barrio spirituality reflects a new way of talking about and experiencing a living relationship with God. Mainstream society's quest culture reveals that many persons are anxiously searching for spiritual depth and meaning for their lives. They stand a good chance of finding it in the cast-aside space of the barrio. Barrio spirituality says the thirst for contact with ultimate reality does not require consuming the latest remedy in the spiritual marketplace; instead, true spiritual depth and social-ethical renewal means finding deliverance in the loving arms of a barrio Jesus who says to proclaim the good news and enact God's will in the world. I think spiritual seekers within and outside of the church will learn from their brothers and sisters in the barrio that the world still belongs to God.

Latinos argue that mainline Christianity does not have to update itself by accommodating the norms of contemporary culture to the point of having no distinctive contribution to make in society. The people of the barrio suggest that the hope and message of the gospel links the quest for meaning with a critique of dominant social, political, economic, and cultural values. As the mainline church has become less appealing to spiritual seekers, its renewal will come by looking for God in the rejected places of society where social problems and inequalities of power too often ignored by mainline piety are visible. In other words, by looking to the barrio as God's own evangelizing witness, the mainline church will reclaim the depth of the gospel by action that leads to a more engaged spirituality and critical theology.

Barrio Christians are energized by the collective imagination of the poor and are keenly aware that whether or not the mainline church is aware of it Jesus walks the stony road. Barrio spirituality is not self-centered, but seeks to link the search for spiritual meaning with striving for "the deeper insight that was in Christ Jesus" (Phil. 2:15), especially by noting that the God who is God of all creation envisions the evangelizing activity of the church to include working for a world without poverty and oppression for human beings. If seeker spirituality within and outside of the church engages the spiritual marketplace with the desire to possess divine truth, barrio faith reminds us that such religious calculations misunderstand the God who is always more, revealed in weakness and already in possession of us.

THE CHURCH

moments alone
sitting in a pew
behind an altar of

wood in a church
white folks left
us after savage

summers waiting
for God to
lead us to life.

thinking of the
people listening
for the sweet

words that will
prompt them from
the shadows to

their feet gripping
street signs with
the Word you send

to carry them beyond
each daily prison
to the promised land.

4

The Good News Politics of Jesus

The beginning of the twenty-first century finds many persons in the United States anxious and insecure about the future. The number of persons who disbelieve positive solutions to social problems can come from schools, politics, the economy, and churches appears to be growing. The airplanes flown into the World Trade Center buildings, the Pentagon, and an open field in Pennsylvania have played no small part in the growing American feeling of despair. In local bookshops and in some congregations during coffee hour people's conversations give credence to Samuel Huntington's thesis that in the post–Cold War world religiously defined civilizations will clash in ways that are violent and enlist the apparatus of the state.[1]

Of course, evangelists once preached that the end of the Cold War would give birth to a less threatening and more positively integrated world. In the 1990s, their euphoria was sparked by the idea of an emerging harmonious world order, but such a view was shattered by the rise in global ethnic and religious violence. In the wake of the September 11 terrorist attacks, national grief now interrupts the conventional understanding that religion is always a force for peace and good in society. Mainline Christians who counted on religion to summon moral power for the good of all people find themselves today sitting at the foot of the cross grappling with silence. Who can believe that pious people motivated by religious belief can use violence and murder to promote their cause? In our post–September 11 world, we are more keenly aware of global interdependency and the evil deprivation creates. As Benjamin Barber notes:

> There are no oceans wide enough to protect a nation from a tainted
> atmosphere or a spreading plague, no walls high enough to defend a
> people against a corrupt ideology or a vengeful prophet, no security
> strict enough to keep a determined martyr from his sacrificial rounds.
> Nor is any nation ever again likely to experience untroubled prosper-
> ity and plenty unless others are given the same opportunity. Suffering
> too has been democratized, and those most likely to experience it will
> find a way to compel those most remote from it to share the pain. If
> there cannot be equity of justice, there will be equity of injustice. . . .
> [This] is the hard lesson of interdependence, taught by terror's
> unsmiling pedagogues.[2]

Since September 11, 2001, many mainline Christians have associated the
cause of Christ with an aggressive war on terrorism and so-called non-Christian
civilization. As the mentality that what is best for America is best for the world
takes greater hold of the mainstream American pulpit, new conditions are created for promoting global and local injustice. The "us" and "them" mentality
evident in public discourse hardly reflects the Christian concern to enact gracious justice in the world; hence, we desperately need to promote alternative
thinking that seeks first to understand how cultures have been produced historically, materially, ideologically, and in interaction with each other.[3] In order
to overcome the mentality that those unlike us are the incarnation of evil,
democratic institutions and political and church leaders will need to encourage a broader knowledge of the world.[4]

Christians who prefer to think faith is irrelevant in politics will need to consider today the meaning of the political vocation of evangelism. President
Bush believes America can "rid the world of evil," but that is an accomplish-
ment that "even God has not succeeded in doing."[5] The White House framed
the global order following September 11 as a battleground of "good versus
evil." White House speech-making reflects the view that the United States is
home to a chosen people whose form of government is nothing less than the
legitimate focus of God's interaction with the world. Although the threat of
terrorism in the world is rooted in structures of injustice and a politics of violence generated by reactionary religion, nine days following the horrific attack
that took thousands of innocent lives, President George W. Bush remarked:

> Americans are asking, why do they hate us? They hate what we see
> right here in this chamber—a democratically elected government.
> Their leaders are self-appointed. They hate our freedoms—our free-
> dom of religion, our freedom of speech, our freedom to vote and
> assemble, and disagree with each other.[6]

Today various theologians and public intellectuals are questioning the new
political theologies of the White House.[7]

Today's evangelists must certainly question the idea that empire building has a role in Christ's mission. What does Christ's command to love our neighbor mean for us today? What does announcing the kingdom of God have to do with our enemies? Will our following of Jesus in a less secure world renew our thinking on politics? Is the church called to be publicly respected, or prophetic? How do we keep the pulpit from being used as an evangelizing mechanism in defense of national culture? What is the Christian stance toward American global power? The structures that now tempt us toward injustice and the systemic forces that make it difficult to produce right relationships require an evangelistic message that enables Christians to take a "critical position over against the self-justifications of those in power."[8] Christian witness cannot but see that God opposes both the spirituality of terrorism and the spirituality of revenge.[9]

Religion has had a long and active relationship to politics in American society, but among many mainline church members one still finds resistance to the idea that politics has anything to do with evangelism.[10] There are Christians who find it difficult to accept the idea that God may call them to a political witness that opposes mainstream political thinking and action; indeed, not too few mainline Christians prefer to stay focused on a theologically shallow and individualistic faith witness.[11] The history of Christianity shows that religious beliefs have been used to legitimize cultures of oppression, and the same beliefs reoriented from the perspective of the victimized have motivated social-critical thinking and prophetic action to bring about progressive social and political changes.[12] Christian politics today should bear witness to the victory of Christ not by encouraging submission to government authority but by standing against unjust suffering, the oppressive arrogance of power, and nationalistic self-interest.[13]

American political and religious leaders are accused by the evangelical left of being captive to a culture that lacks a vision of moral transformation. They object to seeing politics reflect "our worst values of selfishness, greed, divisiveness, fear and power [instead of] our best values of compassion, community, diversity, hope, and service."[14] For this reason, I think the political meaning of evangelism is best discovered when Christians bear witness to the liberating message of Christ in ways that today shape a different world and that critique the current imperial covenant theology. Indeed, the mainline church should more aggressively speak out against the practices that permit our government to become "a franchise of multinational capital" and our political culture "a seller's market in knavery."[15] When the political leadership of the two-party system disconnects historical agency from our best values, the active presence of God's Spirit in the church empowers us to forge a Christian politics that denounces injustices of every kind that keep us from striving toward the fullness of life.

Political evangelization requires debating the will of God in the context of the dehumanizing economic, political, and existential conditions of human beings.[16] It means becoming aware that Christianity has a political message that finds its clearest identity in Jesus, the political agitator from the wrong side of town. Our vision for political evangelism comes from following the One who was rejected and killed by those in society who controlled religion and power. Renewed moral values emerge from trust in the Lord who empowers us to preach and enact the good news, heal fragmented communities (Acts 1:8), love enemies, and pray for persecutors (Matt. 5:44). Jesus' ministry provides us with moral values and an alternative vision of political, economic, social, individual, and religious life. The witness of Jesus teaches us to walk with those who hunger for bread, seek to change power structures, and call on elite leaders to find solutions to unjust suffering with people on the margins and not in boasting about their wisdom and might (Jer. 9:23).

ASPECTS OF THE POLITICS OF FAITH

In recent history, subdivisions of mainline Christian communities have made use of church structures and resources to shape an alternative perception of world community and engage in efforts to build democracy and global justice.[17] Since the civil rights struggle, the symbolic and actual resources of various religious groups have challenged fundamental assumptions about how government devises and implements its domestic and foreign policy. For instance, in the 1960s members of various ethnic communities in the civil rights struggle joined black clergy to transform society's race relations.[18] In the 1970s and 1980s, on issues of war and peace, mainline religious groups demonstrated their solidarity with Latino Christians who were resisting state-sponsored terror and exploitation in Central America, declaring sanctuary for Central American refugees, engaging in nonviolent defense of human rights, and advocating the cancellation of unpaid third-world debt.[19] At the same time, the new Christian Right was actively influencing American political life along conservative values. What is clear is that the links between religion and politics have not always been synonymous with accommodation to the social order.[20]

Mainline religious communities' renewed sense of political agency is part of a global revival of religion that began in the second half of the twentieth century.[21] Intellectual elites who predicted the retreat of religion from public life in view of economic and social modernization, rationalization, and progressive and humanistic values had it wrong. Those who argued that the fate of religion was to adapt to secular society and eventually decline were surprised when a religious resurgence unfolded that called for the recovery of the sacred as the center of social, political, economic, and cultural life.[22] Presently, the return of religion is evident in the workplace, in ordinary affairs, and in the concerns of politics and foreign affairs; indeed, in countries around the globe the "unsecularization of the world is one of the dominant social facts."[23]

In America, the return of religion has issued forth in the form of a new civil religious nationalism.[24] For instance, it was not uncommon for President Clinton to make public requests for forgiveness, open cabinet meetings with prayer, consult regularly with pastors, attend prayer breakfasts, meet with religious leaders around the country, remark on religious themes of the Bible, and work diligently to promote the free exercise of religion.[25] During Clinton's presidency, Congress passed an extensive piece of legislation called the Religious Freedom Restoration Act (RFRA), which addressed the free exercise of religion in the federal workplace, public schools, and foreign policy. Clinton, who signed the bill, considered the free exercise of religion "perhaps the most precious of all American liberties."[26]

Stephen Carter's book *The Culture of Disbelief* influenced Clinton with its thesis that religion has been sidelined in American political life. Clinton embraced Carter's argument that democracy and political discourse would be better served if religion were a more open participant in public life.[27] Subsequently, Clinton integrated religious groups into the agenda-setting of his administration, enabling them to engage in social debate on the grounds of their religion. Clinton identified faith with being American to such a degree that he believed one could not lead the nation without the truth that comes at the church altar rail. Although the Clinton presidency brought different faiths together to advance public policy, his treatment of religion as a force for good avoided mention of the religious motivation of white supremacist and hate groups.

During the 2000 presidential campaign, Al Gore, Joseph Lieberman, and George W. Bush openly discussed their faith and its influence on their decisions in public office. For example, Bush talked about how he had "recommitted his life to Christ," Al Gore told the press that the "purpose of my life is to glorify God," and Joseph Lieberman argued strongly for a public role for religion.[28] After the tragic events of September 11, members of congress sang "God Bless America" on the Capitol steps, bumper stickers combined displays of patriotism with a call for God's blessing and guidance, and special services around the country reminded citizens of the sacred status of the nation. By 2003, a new religious nationalism reasserted the United States is God's chosen and just nation, which reflects the ideology that makes us, as Reinhold Niebuhr once observed, "the most innocent nation on earth."[29]

During the 2004 presidential campaign, pollsters reported that most Americans prefer not to vote on the basis of a candidate's religious affiliation, but more than a third of eligible voters believe it important to consider the religious views of a presidential candidate. Because religion matters in political campaigning, John Kerry visited a St. Louis church during his presidential campaign and after quoting from James 2:14 asked, "When we look at what is happening in America today, where are the works of compassion?"[30] George W. Bush has spoken publicly of his coming to Jesus as an adult in the context of a men's Bible study group, his decision to quit drinking, and his belief that God has a plan for him and America.[31] Of course, the statements of both men pale next to those made by Jerry Falwell and Pat Robertson, who declared the September 11 terrorist attacks were punishment from God for America's sin, especially attributable to gays, lesbians, feminists, abortionists, the ACLU, and People for the American Way.[32]

Although some mainline Christians do pray today for swords not to be drawn to resolve conflicts, not nearly enough of them pray for God to turn weapons into plowshares.[33] In post–September 11 America, a new religious nationalism that deceptively attributes sacred power to the state is creating a strong impulse in congregations to seek a strong homeland defense over the gospel imperatives to love, especially to love one's enemies.[34] The moral rhetoric of the White House demonstrates a desire to bring us to the conviction that the defense of "our freedoms" and the will of God are the same.[35] The carefully crafted lies that support today's unprincipled politics, however, show that "ideology represses nothing; it simply blinds with light."[36] Still, social reality does not permit us to equate loyalty to God with uncritical acceptance of the organization of state power, or to confuse the president's decisions for our lives with those of God.[37] The U.S. response to the post–September 11 global reality requires admission that

> the arrogant U.S. Achilles, having defeated his Russian foe Hector, continues to grind the vanquished foe into the dust and humiliate him. A much lesser adversary has let fly the arrows that have wounded Achilles seriously at his most vulnerable spot. Flushed with overweening pride, Achilles is lashing out at all his adversaries at once, deluding himself that he can protect his heel by wearing combat boots.[38]

Unquestionably, the new religious nationalism has roots in the early history of the civil religious tradition.[39] This civil religious tradition expressed explanatory values and ideas about the origin of the American people and what they stand for.[40] In other words, as a culturally established meaning system steeped in biblical symbolism (e.g., chosen people, promised land, new Jerusalem, city set on a hill, death and resurrection), the American civil religious tradition stood alongside denominational and ethnic boundaries seeking to create a people of common values, identity, and conscience out of diversity.[41] As the ultimate concerns of American society came into play and its fundamental ideas about basic values were challenged, Americans found solace in a civil religious tradition that stepped in to control the uncontrollable and restore a sense of meaningful order to life.[42]

With roots in traditional civil religion, what can be expected of the new religious nationalism? First, it will draw on imagined truths of society and use a tradition of beliefs, symbols, and rituals to shape thinking and acting in public life. It will retell the story of how God chose the United States to be the "ark of salvation" and the bearer of freedom for oppressed peoples of the world. Second, it will find new ways to enable people to attach strong religious sentiments to Independence Day, Memorial Day, Thanksgiving, the American flag, presidential birthdays, inaugurations, and September 11 civil ceremonies and commemorative events. Mainline church pulpits influenced by the new religious nationalism will voice the values of the dominant political system and its myths of collective identity.[43] The new religious nationalism will be a loyal advisor of power, prestige, and the American way.[44] Nonetheless, the mainline church's political witness of Christ should not let its members forget that "Christianity did not come into being as a national religion. . . . It does not bind the hearts of citizens to the state, but lures them away from it."[45]

As civil religion serves up religious nationalism and uncritical patriotism, many mainline Christians easily forget the horrors of war in Europe, Korea, Japan, Vietnam, Central Asia, the Middle East, Bosnia, Rwanda, Guatemala, El Salvador, and Nicaragua, among others. The new religious nationalism tells us that God is more interested in law and order than justice and love. This religious viewpoint places God at the service of the government, its leaders, and its laws. As a form of blatant idolatry, it fills people with a self-righteousness that distances them from the God of Jesus Christ who "brings princes to naught, and makes the rulers of the earth as nothing" (Isa. 40:23). Because the new religious nationalism has recently focused on the Middle East and terrorism, mainline church leaders who wish to counter the nationalistic views of God can do so by honestly discussing our role in the region. As Edward Said notes:

> For two generations the United States has sided in the Middle East mostly with tyranny and injustice. No struggle for democracy, or women's rights, or secularism and the rights of minorities has the United States officially supported. Instead one administration after another has propped up compliant and unpopular clients, turned away from the efforts of small peoples to liberate themselves from military occupation, while subsidizing their enemies. . . . Loyalty and patriotism should be based on a critical sense of what the facts are, and what,

as residents of this shrinking and depleted planet, Americans owe their neighbors and the rest of mankind.[46]

For years Latin American authoritarian regimes operated with the support of the government of the United States. These regimes used murder and state terrorism to repress tens of thousands of Christians, who questioned the meaning of political systems that produced hunger, exploitation, economic inequality, and separation of the poor from the decisions affecting their daily lives.[47] The grisly terrorist act of September 11 is a reminder that the twentieth century opened with the Armenian genocide in Turkey, the murder of Orthodox clergy by Stalin in Russia, Christians killing Christians in two world wars and in Central American wars, the United States dropping atomic bombs on Japanese cities and placing Japanese Americans in concentration camps at home, Hitler and German culture Christianity sponsoring Jewish genocide, and wars in Southeast Asia, Africa, and the Middle East. Indeed, terrorism was never the product of a single ideology or economic system.[48] In the face of contemporary suffering and injustice, mainline Christians may not forget that "all sufferers can find comfort in the solidarity of the Crucified; but only those who struggle against evil by following the example of the Crucified will discover him at their side."[49]

The witness of Martin Luther King Jr. speaks to the narrow-mindedness inherent in the new religious nationalism. His prophetic civil religion drew the attention of Americans to a God of truth who called into question society's offenses in light of the situation of trampled people and in terms of national ideals. King challenged the nation to live up to its deepest vision of democracy, equality, and justice by changing its perception of domestic and international social relations.[50] He challenged religious nationalism by calling on America to cultivate a nonimperialist global perspective on world community, combine scientific and technological progress with moral and spiritual development, eradicate racism, and choose nonviolence as a means of domestic and global change.[51] He believed God ultimately breaks into history to overcome the moral limitations of human beings.[52]

If we are to oppose the new religious nationalism's misguided worldview and avoid following its "warrior Jesus," the removal of our patriotic blinders must be achieved by listening to those who suffer in situations of oppression, exploitation, and ideological bondage and who condemn pious support for international conflicts and capitalist structures of global domination.[53] The post–September 11 world calls on mainline Christians to rediscover Jesus in evangelizing action that addresses twisted values and all politics of death with the righteousness of the gospel. As Cornel West observes, "The great dramatic battle of the twenty-first century is the dismantling of empire and the deepening of democracy."[54] The empire-shattering kingdom of God that draws near requires learning from the socially rejected (Luke 7:32–50; 14:13), loving our enemies, and choosing nonviolent action in struggles to achieve new life in society. Today's religious nationalists and government officials who believe their decisions are God's decisions should remember that Jesus said, "Not everyone who says to me, 'Lord, Lord,' will enter the kingdom of heaven, but only the one who does the will of my Father in heaven" (Matt. 7:21).

THE POLITICS OF JESUS

Does Jesus provide us with a model of good news for politics? What was Jesus' stance toward the politics and practices of the religious and political leaders of his day? How did Jesus' understanding of relationship with God place him in conflict with established religious and political authorities? For mainline Christians who argue that nothing in Jesus' ministry has the character of dealing with political affairs, Jesus' hanging from the cross at Golgotha suggests another observation. For those who argue that Jesus calls on us to submit to political authorities, the prophetic ministry of Jesus asks them to imagine alternative possibilities for life that create political spaces not determined by a culture of fear, religious nationalism, or the will for power. The reign of God announced by Jesus draws us into a new story of politics—of just relationships, love, and self-giving. Let us examine aspects of the gospel accounts that show the political evangelism of Jesus, the One who disobeyed rules and political authorities.[55]

Marcus Borg observes that a great deal of twentieth-century scholarship concerned with the mission and teaching of Jesus did not locate traditions about him in political contexts showing Jesus' concern with the institutional life of Israel and the political threat of Roman colonialism. Instead of examining Jesus in relationship to groups, history, and politics, scholars before the 1970s largely excluded political questions from their examination of the Jesus tradition. These scholars thought Jesus was unconcerned with politics and that his ministry was focused on timeless moral truths unconditioned by the political conflicts in Roman-occupied Palestine.[56] In fact, the ministry of Jesus took place in the historical setting of Israel's conflict with Rome and Jesus' conflict with Jewish leaders concerning his alternative vision of structures and social relationships in Jewish society.[57]

The politics of Jesus points beyond how members of society secure their common good by exercising public power and distributing economic goods. By "the politics of Jesus" I refer to the attempt to discover Christ in what we do and how we give meaning to evangelism in our lives. The logic of this politics urges members of mainline churches to expand their circle of compassion beyond the familiar terrain of relationships to those who are demeaned by the practices of a social system characterized by an ethos of selfishness and materialism.[58] The politics of Jesus calls us to live beyond our self-interest and allegiances that idolize power and wealth, and it permits us to find God in the requirement of loving each other. The logic of evangelism here means being present to others while aware of the transcendent reality of God that holds our thinking, feeling, and acting accountable to divine standards of compassion (1 John 4:8).

Jesus' brand of politics was deeply concerned with the structures and norms of society that define the nature of historical community. He was at odds with the piety of the status quo, which disregarded the need to build a life together that offered greater justice, love, and life for those denied the right to it (see Luke 10:29–37; 11:37–54; Mark 1:41; 2:23–28; 7:11–12; John 4:27). Jesus defied religious and political leaders who supported pathologies of power based on the idea that God is on the side of injustice. His politics gave voice to a gospel that called for sociopolitical transformation based on lovingkindness. His ministry exposed the theological ideas and religious nationalism that justified elite social power and promoted exclusionary practices (Mark 8:12; 10:3; 12:35). He also evangelized by teaching followers to confront power with the good news that transforms society with the alternative values of equality, peace, freedom, dignity, love, and compassion (Luke 22:12–15).[59]

Politics in the image of Christ seeks to gather and direct history toward the larger vision of life offered by God. Jesus does not make things right and whole by commanding us to separate faith from political life; indeed, those who follow Jesus in obedience are filled with the awareness that Christian political acting and thinking rest on the ultimate hope of the coming reign of God, where death is swallowed up in victory (1 Cor. 15:54). I think Jesus had a very clear vision of the relationship of faith to politics, which he taught to his disciples in the prayer that envisions God's will done on earth as in heaven. This prayer provides a rationale for acting in the world of power politics, and one can imagine its political effect did not escape Jesus' followers when one realizes that "heaven . . . then as now, was, and is, in very good shape . . . [and] earth, then as now, . . . was, and is, problematic."[60]

The evangelism of the crucified Lord teaches us to read the Scriptures and guide life in terms of oppositional political frameworks of consciousness. For instance, when Mary speaks about God in the Magnificat, the core idea of her song is the power of a God who acts in history through saving actions that reverse inequalities in the social order. Mary's song points to a set of political ideas such as the liberating power of God, problems with the social arrangements in society, and human hope in the coming of the One who breaks the economic and political conditions holding people in bondage. In other words,

Mary's song announces the political idea that "the social task of the future is equality . . . the equality that springs from recognition of other people and the reparation due to our victims."[61]

As we understand our role within a biblical framework of political consciousness, it becomes possible to evangelize the wider society by questioning wars for control of resources, deteriorating race relations, and growing polarization between the rich and poor in the world. The power of the gospel Jesus commands us to proclaim interprets the meaning of political society with the countercultural viewpoint of concern for crucified peoples and self-emptying for the sake of others. Jesus, who experienced marginality, condemnation, abuse, and finally death at the hands of powerful groups, taught that discipleship is a political commitment geared to working for the life on earth promised by God (Matt. 5:1–12; Luke 6:20–36). This means that following the crucified Lord requires of the church a discipleship of peacemaking and resistance to all structures that dehumanize people.

The political significance of Jesus' ministry contradicts wretched conditions of life, opposes profit systems that condemn people to death, and supports human actions that defend against the escalating violence against creation. Following Jesus in the name of the God who suffers, acts, and overcomes death means the church proclaims the world cannot be separated from God's will for it. In a world ruled by the idolatry of money, threatened by nuclear annihilation, ravaged by racial hatred, and endangered by increasing levels of poverty, walking with Jesus requires a costly discipleship that bears witness to the God who overcomes this politics of death in defense of life. In short, the politics of Jesus leads to evangelizing action that calls us to build communities that overcome all kinds of injustice and that reject antagonisms based on race, class, and gender.[62]

THE MINISTRY OF COMPASSION

Jesus invited the destitute, outcasts, and the rich into the reign of God and advocated compassion as a basic framework for structuring relationships and institutions. There are, of course, many Christians who believe Jesus' acts of compassion were purely religious in nature and too focused on the imminent end of this world to have any relevance for action to promote changes in political society. They may even insist that the Roman inscription above the head of the crucified Christ, "Jesus Nazarenus Rex Judaeorum," is the product of a misunderstanding.[63] In my view, the inscription above the cross means that Jesus was killed because the Roman authorities understood that he wanted to change the established system of domination.[64]

EASTER VISIT

we have come
into the church

after years of death
lived in a world

no longer listening
to God. the incense

cleanses our wounds
as flickering candles

show us the way back.
we sit before two sore

eyes on a saint never
suspicious of strangers,

full of acceptance. we
light candles for those

remaining a voice
in dusty ash to

raise them from
the terrible silence.

The political evangelism of Jesus was expressed in a compassionate ministry that questioned life-denying structures and offered a challenging alternative vision of life together.[65] Jesus' ethic of compassion broke with the vicious circles of cultural understanding that alienated human beings from each other and the God of radical acceptance. He moved away from the conventional understanding expressed in the Jewish purity system that structured social life into a polarized system where people were defined as clean or unclean. He rejected the politics of the purity system that created a social world with sharp boundaries between categories of people: rich and poor, male and female, righteous and sinner.[66] He shifted the priorities of faith from human approaches to God based on observance of rules to the God who approaches human beings with a promise of transformed life.[67]

In Jesus' day, the political dimensions of the purity system were defined by what was believed to be God-given arrangements that were upheld by the mainline religious authorities and the political elites associated with the temple. Because the temple was a central symbol of economic, political, and religious interests, the "politics of purity was to some extent the ideology of the dominant elites—religious, political and economic."[68] But Jesus revealed that God had no need for a purity system or the sociopolitical order connected to it. This is demonstrated in Jesus' shifting of the sociopolitical paradigm by defying the purity rules and demonstrating God's ongoing activity by healing persons who were culturally and structurally marginalized (e.g., lepers [Mark 1:40–45; Luke 17:11–19], the woman with a hemorrhage [Mark 5:25–34], the paralytic [Mark 2:1–12], the man with a withered hand [Mark 3:1–6]).

Jesus taught that religious rules were not capable of making people experience God; rather, God was accessible through men, women, and children who were socially outcast, felt unworthy, and suffered great need. In the name of the God who cares about establishing human relations, Jesus challenged the direction of his society; broke table fellowship taboos; defied Sabbath, debt, and purity rules; and criticized the prevailing ideology of the temple.[69] Naturally, Jesus came into conflict with society's power groups because "in those days as in our own, society would tolerate a preaching about 'God' that did not entail a prophetic denunciation of the basic sin of injustice."[70] But Jesus continued to teach followers that God was not a harsh judge who divided the world into the righteous and sinners; instead, Jesus revealed God as a loving parent who questioned the mainstream piety that overlooked the lesson from history that "when God hears the cry of the oppressed [God] emerges from [God's] own history (cf. Ex. 3:9; 6:5)."[71]

Jesus was aware that the Zealots, Pharisees, Essenes, and Sadducees imagined the restoration of Israel, but he was critical of the way their exclusionary religious views contributed to discrimination and oppression in society.[72] His mission called for a change in established cultural attitudes in order to draw religious and economic elites close to those who always cry out that human society needs to be in harmony with the will of God. Thus, Jesus' ministry demystified the politically consequent idea that God requires ideological, social, and economic stratification in society. Jesus made it clear to his followers that what happens in the world is directly related to how they choose to live their lives. If the religious and political authorities plotted to kill Jesus for practicing compassion to the least among people (Mark 3:6), his followers were asked not to negate the practice of mercy that reflected a radical trust in God's presence in the world.[73]

The compassionate ministry of Jesus moved people away from routine piety toward a clearer understanding of the God who takes sides. His ministry did not establish a new set of rules by which to divide the world in terms of insiders and outsiders; instead, he invited people to stop living entirely on their own terms and to enter the reign of God, where the existentially blind, crippled, diseased, and dead received sight, walked, and knew full life (Matt. 11:2–6; Luke 7:22–23). By associating his ministry with the social themes of Isaiah (Luke 4:18–19), a distinctive message was sent to established leaders about the God who announces blessing to the poor (Luke 6:20–21) and woe to the rich (Luke 6:24–25). Not surprisingly, Jesus died at the hands of religious and political leaders who felt challenged by this political work at the edge of society.[74] He died for defying traditional piety's holiness rules and building a community of authentic inclusion.

Jesus was not an apolitical teacher who sent followers out to dispense a message of individual improvement. This Palestinian Jewish prophet held that the best way to fulfill the will of God was to restore the dignity of outcasts (Luke 10:4; 12:22–24), oppose the structural oppression of women (Luke 7:11–17; 8:1–3, 10:38–42; 13:10–13; 16:18), avoid the idolization of wealth (Luke 8:14; 16:15; 18:24–25; 21:1–4), and stay connected to suffering people (Luke 10:29–37). Jesus invited followers to meet him in the hungry, imprisoned, homeless, and sick (Matt. 25; Luke 14:15–25) by embracing a political vocation that practiced a social solidarity that worked to end unjust structures in the world. But he warned followers that compassionate living results in persecution at the hands of political authorities (Luke 21:12–15).

As mainline churches evangelize, they will need to take seriously the call to compassion by finding God beyond verbal statements about the renewal of life and solemn Sunday worship. Empowered by the risen Christ, Christians can live more compassionately and engage in a new lifestyle of solidarity with those whose truth is denied by the controlling culture. Christians who seek to embody the politics of Jesus act compassionately in the world to socially transform the institutions and structures governed by the logic of greed and indifference. By living more mercifully and radically in the gospel, mainline churches will more fully create bridges between individuals, cultural communities, and institutions reflective of political impulses that let divided old worlds die and a new world of unity come into being (Rom. 12:1–2).[75]

For Christians living in what is arguably the most powerful nation in the world a first step in the direction of compassionate living and political evangelization is to seek solidarity with crucified people in the barrio and world who are denied dignity, hope, and life and too often regard their very lives as a curse.[76] In *The Politics of Compassion*, written during the height of U.S.-sponsored wars in Central America, Jack Nelson-Pallmeyer discusses what a simple lifestyle change would mean for North American Christians seeking to embody Jesus' politics of compassion. Drawing on the insights of Jörgen Lissner, then the secretary of peace and human rights for the Lutheran Federation in Geneva, Switzerland, Pallmeyer suggests a simple lifestyle is meaningful

> *as an act of faith* performed against the mind-polluting effects of over-consumption; *as an act of withdrawal* from the achievement-neurosis of our high pressure materialist societies; *as an act of solidarity* with the majority of humankind, those who have no choice about lifestyle; *as an act of sharing* with others what has been given to us, or of returning what has been stolen by us through unjust social and economic structures; *as an act of celebration* of the riches found in creativity, spirituality, and community with others rather than in mindless materialism; *as an act of provocation* . . . to arouse curiosity leading to dialogue with others about affluence, alienation, poverty, and social injustice; *as an act of anticipation* of the era when the self-confidence and assertiveness of the underprivileged force new power relationships and new patterns of resource allocation upon us; *as an act of advocacy* of legislated changes in present patterns of production and consumption in the direction of a new international economic order; *as an exercise of purchasing power* to redirect production away from the satisfaction of artificially created wants toward a supply of goods and services that meet genuine needs.[77]

Christians who commit themselves to build a church that lives beyond the limitations of the present order and its "self-interest" know that the future of society is a matter of politics. Only a new incarnation of faith that engages political life for the sake of the reign of God will bring the lifestyle changes for which the world longs. Historically, some Christians have participated in the truth of Jesus Christ by entering the political arena and contesting it with the alternative vision of life revealed by the gospel. These disciples are aware that

Jesus' compassionate ministry always points to the saving activity of God, who calls human beings to make the message of God's reign credible. By firmly believing in Jesus and working confidently with the crucified among whom Jesus died, the groundwork is laid to evangelize society and ultimately overcome idolatrous political and economic systems.

CONCLUSION

The political evangelism of Jesus was revealed the instant divine love became flesh and worked toward bringing more dignity and justice into the world. As a political community, the mainline church stands before powers and principalities and hears the word of God that says, "For there is still a vision for the appointed time." (Hab. 2:3). In other words, the people of God do not line up with those who disbelieve positive solutions to life's complicated problems can be found. In the post–September 11 world, those who pursue the compassionate work of Jesus do not spiritualize revenge, yield moral ground to the new religious nationalism, or ignore how global structures of injustice ensure the democratization of suffering. Christian political sensibilities and the conditions of the church's evangelism are grounded in the poor, the racially despised, and all people who hunger for bread, justice, life, and human dignity.

In a less secure world, many American political leaders support their national vision with a new religious nationalism that appears to place God at the service of government. This public expression of the sacred leaves very little room to prophetically critique established government policies and defy the logic of domination constitutive of practical political and economic life. Nonetheless, Christian politics is the effort to live the truth of Jesus Christ in the public square and the concern about how to find God in a world marked by sin and injustice. Christians are not apologists of the state, but persons seeking Christ in what they think and do. The logic of Jesus' politics urges us to live consciously in society and to engage controversial issues of power that unjustly structure institutions and relationships. Mainline congregations that embody the compassion of Christ resist the temptation of retreating from the world.

Finally, the politics of Jesus suggests that changing the historic structuring of institutions and relationships in society requires that the symbolic expression and compassionate ministry of the church publicly challenge established political views of truth. In the case of Christian political witness, this means making room for the experience and insights of nonpersons, the people unmade by economies of power, ideologies of domination, and the daily practices of injustice. In the final analysis, imagining the vision that awaits its time requires nothing less than anticipating the renewal of the social order by way of words and deeds grounded in the good news of Christ.

PIECE WORK

God knows where all
the fake jewelry went
that our young Puerto Rican

mothers assembled sitting
around the kitchen table
talking of old dreams and

memories of the island. they
all believed in miracles
and never forgot to pray in

Spanish so all heaven
above the streets of the
South Bronx could hear.

Ana's swollen stomach moved
then with a life inside
already well-fed by love

in a world of little bread.
in the other room children
laughed at television shows

featuring people who looked
different and happily wrestled
away the very time which one

day would hand them to
afflictions too great for
debating truth with God.

one cloudy night a mother
died after a long illness
a piece of custom jewelry

shaped like an angel was
placed on her burial dress
for the final long good-bye.

the kitchen table-talk was
not the same nor the other
room so noisy. . . .

5

The Church in a World Apart

Mainline Christians who gather on Sunday morning affirm in their creeds the "catholicity" of the church with increased awareness that the community surrounding them is culturally diverse. Yet many of the congregations they belong to prefer to separate themselves from their local contexts and protect their boundaries from the people outside, who are presumed to be not "our kind of people." School desegregation, affirmative action, and government policies have contributed to reducing racial and ethnic inequality in American society, but the vast majority of the approximately 300,000 Christian congregations in the United States, or nearly 90 percent, are constituted by one racial group.[1] In other words, one can still say Sunday morning is America's segregated hour.[2]

The post-1965 immigration has made mainline congregations aware of the challenge of cultural pluralism, which necessitates adopting an evangelizing viewpoint that promotes diversity and recognizes the right of others to live as they wish.[3] The sign of the times means evangelism involves proclaiming the good news of Christ in different ways within a pluralistic society. Congregational studies have empirically shown that mainline churches that are inclusive of other cultures and ethnic groups positively influence racial attitudes and break down the ethnic stereotypes of their members. Mainline congregations engaging in evangelism that promotes intercultural cooperation, racial reconciliation, and ethnic equality typically acquire renewed resources with which to embody a richer history, spirituality, and theological imagination.

Cultural diversity has always been a part of the national experience in the United States, but the histories lived by Native Americans, Asians, African

Americans, and Latinos show that ethnic and racial diversity was mostly unappreciated by white society, and the cultural achievements and traditions of nonwhite groups were mostly unrecognized. As the question of cultural pluralism comes to the forefront of Christian experience, the concern to more critically reflect on the self-disclosure of God and the study of human beings in their diversity will emerge for local congregations. Evangelistic activities taking place across racial, cultural, class, and linguistic boundaries will afford a deeper understanding of the God who molds, shapes, and reshapes in different cultural settings a people's ideas, values, attitudes, explanations, and rules for living.

Currently in the United States, cultural diversity is evidenced in people's different styles of dress, thinking, speaking, and acting. Yet evangelism is thought best pursued on the basis of a homogenous principle that avoids racial, cultural, and linguistic variation.[4] The homogenous principle overlooks how in Christ the early church overcame barriers to cross-cultural communication and community life; indeed, God's truth is upheld when the church evangelizes people in their cultural reality.[5] The core value of making disciples of all nations (Matt. 28:19) expressed in the Great Commission was never a mandate to avoid or eradicate differences. Hence, the Christian message necessarily means acting in ways that promote respect for people from other cultures and "proclaiming everything we have understood about God to people in many contexts" (Matt. 28:20).[6]

Evangelism must now aim to give us a church that reconciles the world and turns it upside down by communicating the good news of the God who created the rich variety of human beings. In part, today this means recollecting that the early church did not grow on the basis of a principle of uniformity, but "the early Christian movement reached out for the very purpose of creating and encompassing incredible diversity within the larger reach of God's reconciling unity."[7] Across the ancient world and within the auspices of the Roman Empire, the early Christian movement encompassed ethnic and language groups. Followers of Jesus Christ acted on the commitment to break down walls that kept people from east, west, north, and south antagonistically apart. In other words, Jesus called a new community into being from "every tribe and language and people and nation" (Rev. 5:9).

The New Testament authors reflect how the God of reconciliation who brings down dividing walls of hostility motivates a life of "ungrudging service" concerned with human existence and the future of the world.[8] The obvious feature of the early Christian community is that membership expanded by a focus on Christ and the concern to cut across boundaries of difference. The early Christian movement knew a God of radical inclusiveness, as reflected at Pentecost when a diverse array of human beings arrived in Jerusalem and heard the disciples praise God in their own languages (Acts 2:5–11). Christians followed Jesus by loving their enemies and living a life of humility, unselfish service, and forgiveness toward others in their multicultural world.[9] For this reason, God's vision for the church does not include evangelistic strategies that define community on the basis of avoiding persons unlike the members of one's own group.

In a world where violence and hostility are all too common, Christians who build cross-cultural bridges will better understand the multiple ways God enters into relationship with human beings. As theologian Ron Sider expresses it, "When the church models a new reality that transcends the brokenness of surrounding society, it leavens the whole social order."[10] Evangelism that deepens understanding of cultural diversity influences human values and behavior in ways that can enable one to overcome the tendency to make one's culture the norm to measure all others. Cross-cultural relationships heighten awareness of the identity of individual members of a social group, which permits one to see each cultural subject thinking, feeling, acting, and experiencing life in light of a unique set of encoded meanings about divine reality.[11]

The Word made flesh in the person of Jesus of Nazareth reveals the forward-moving history in which God meets all human beings. Although the gospel is embodied in a particular language and culture, Christians are challenged by it to enter the world to bear witness to the God who continually speaks the truth afresh. What is needed in Christian discipleship is a discernment within which our thinking and acting can affirm that grace binds us to a God who continually judges us by way of strangers. If the cross of Christ reminds us that culturally structured political and economic systems reflect sin in the world, the risen Lord who appeared to his disciples on the road to Emmaus in the form of a stranger makes plain that the good news makes "all things new" in a union that brings people together in allegiance to God's alternative vision for life.

Evangelism today is required to imagine new possibilities for human relationship not based on narrow understandings of community; thus, congregations are challenged to articulate evangelistic strategies in ways that bear witness to God's entering all human contexts.[12] Christians who assemble to proclaim the gospel are a foretaste of a redeemed creation and the embodiment of a prophetic movement in divided social contexts when they open their church doors and set their Communion tables more and more to welcome the excluded. In the long term, cross-cultural evangelistic strategies will change the value-forming cultural practices that currently ensure the heartbreaking racial, ethnic, and class antagonisms in American society. Although these strategies may not result in a dramatic change, over time they will advance cultural shifts in belief and behavior that recognize a greater meaning: the right of all to life given by God.

The incorporation of diverse cultural perspectives into congregational life is not easily accomplished. Church leaders concerned to understand how cultural diversity is foundational for their theological identity need to examine the symbols and narratives that determine how they interpret cultural experience and shape behavior toward people from other cultural groups. Simply renting the church space to another cultural group or occasionally sharing worship experiences will not fully bear witness to the reconciling love of God. Because the gospel requires of the assembled people of God a radical reimaging of social reality, developing a cross-cultural theological awareness and sustained social relationships is necessary to understand that "our well-being and that of the world depend on our acknowledgment and acceptance of ourselves as a small part of creation but integrally related to each part of the created whole."[13] I will now outline ways to understand culture to help in the evangelizing task.

UNDERSTANDING CULTURE

Christ invites the local church to proclaim good news and "the potentialities of life that have not yet come into being,"[14] but this message is to be shared in a racially and ethnically changing society. In many communities around the country, cultural newcomers often understand such institutions as the family, neighborhood, religion, society, and self-identity in ways unlike that of members of the established Euro-American culture. Because the reign of God is radically inclusive and is lived by diverse peoples, mainline congregations moving into the pluralist reality of this century need to understand the meaning of culture. Mainline churches seeking to evangelize local communities should carefully examine what God is doing in diverse contexts where persons make use of cultural ideas, values, and patterns of behavior to negotiate their world.

As the leaders of mainline churches seriously seek to create communities that hope in the coming reign of God, they will find ways to enable congregational members to come to terms with the way God draws the world into community by self-disclosing in the particular time and space of cultures. This means mainline churches will need to produce evangelistic strategies that develop an adequate level of *cross-cultural competence*, which is "the ability to think, feel, and act in ways that acknowledge, respect, and build upon ethnic, [socio]cultural, and linguistic diversity."[15] To this end, I turn our attention to techniques of cultural analysis to present what they offer congregations for developing cross-cultural competence for evangelism.

Current demographic shifts in U.S. society suggest racial and cultural diversity will open up new social-relational worlds for mainline churches, which they will not be able to ignore in their evangelizing witness. As a consequence of higher birthrates among immigrant groups and migration from mostly non-European societies, by the middle of this century most members of American society will trace their historical roots either to Latin America, Africa, Asia, the Middle East, and the Pacific Islands. This emerging diversity is already impacting the nation's neighborhoods, politics, and religious communities, and it leaves little room to doubt that mainline churches will need to become more knowledgeable about the assumptions, attributes, and norms of different cultural groups.[16]

Transportation and communication technologies have greatly reduced the physical and social distances that once thoroughly separated people from different cultural backgrounds. Subsequently, Christians have come to understand that bridging the cultural divide requires affirming that human beings fashion diverse ways of belief, practice, and knowledge to create sustaining ways of life. More and more, Christians who find God today in the barrio, in the poor and oppressed, in cultures seeking alternatives to a broken world, concede that theological awareness of diversity issues forth from the belief that the Christ who gave the disciples the Great Commission requires the gospel message be spoken in many voices.[17] Effective evangelism motivates interest in relating the gospel message to the real dramas of life that are played out within and across cultural contexts.

In order to communicate across lines of cultural difference, local church members will benefit from having a definition of culture that empowers them to grasp and apply basic principles of cultural analysis. Anthropologist Clifford Geertz defines culture as a "historically transmitted pattern of meanings embodied in symbols . . . by means of which men can communicate, perpetuate and develop their own knowledge about and attitudes towards life."[18] According to Geertz, culture is learned behavior common to a social group that provides individuals with a comprehensive way of thinking, feeling and acting in their world. In light of Geertz's definition, one could say that the things taken for granted by us and that provide us with a picture of actuality are nothing less than patterns of learned meaning and behavior.

As an anthropologist, I believe social scientific tools help us critically examine culture and its role in the interpretation of history and individual, social, economic, political, and religious behavior. But what is anthropology? How can it help the evangelizing work of the church? How does it help mainline Christians engage in cross-cultural relationships? Because anthropology studies human diversity, it is relevant to our everyday lives in a multicultural world. For cultural anthropologists, the striking differences in behavior seen from one society to another are examples of different kinds of acquired belief and behavior (cultural knowledge). As James Spradley and David McCurdy note:

When a Toda woman from south India reaches physical maturity, she marries a group of brothers. A Bunyoro man from Africa first marries when he is about 35 years old and thereafter acquires as many more wives as he can afford. In the recent past the Jale of Highland New Guinea ate the enemies they killed in combat; American soldiers in Vietnam piled them up and counted them. . . . Many young American couples employ chemical, mechanical, and surgical means to limit family size; in rural India a man and his wife remember the gods faithfully to ensure the birth of many healthy offspring. A president of the United States buries the family dog in a carefully manicured cemetery plot complete with headstone and sentimental epitaph; a Bontok Ingolot from the Philippines divides his canine with the members of his family at dinner.[19]

Cross-cultural awareness helps us appreciate that our particular culture is just one way of life and adaptation strategy to environmental and social conditions among the thousands of linguistic and cultural possibilities represented by human beings. Local churches engaging in the process of cultural analysis and relationships with other social groups should bear in mind that culture is (1) a socially established structure of meaning through which people interpret their experience and act in the world, (2) a meaning context in which belief, values, behavior, social events, institutions, and worldviews are intelligibly explained, and (3) the product of a particular human group to be grasped in its particularity and in terms of global processes of connection and change.

Cultural identity consists of the behavior patterns and meaning system of a particular social group that is shaped and amended by social interaction over time. In other words, persons in a social group create an identity that informs others to what cultural group they are related. Additionally, cultural variation of beliefs, attitudes, and behaviors exist in every social group due to factors such as ethnicity, race, gender, class, educational level, immigration, place of residence, and exceptional historical events.[20] For this reason, local church groups engaged in cross-cultural evangelism with a specific social group about which they know little or nothing should pay attention to internal cultural variation.

By engaging in cross-cultural relationships, local congregations will discover what is essential to the message of Christ and what is culturally conditioned. In addition, taking other cultures seriously will (1) foster in members of the local church a clearer understanding of why individuals from other cultural groups act in certain ways, (2) provide insight into the knowledge and value systems that sustain behavior in a contact community, and (3) help local churches establish a framework of cross-culturally competent communication that recognizes the "naturalness" of other ways of life. As members of the local church take seriously the terrain of difference in daily life, they will better understand that cultures are complex systems that structure society and ensure that individuals and social groups act in ways considered appropriate. As Charles Taber observes in *The World Is Too Much with Us*:

> Human beings require water and nutrition, so each culture defines certain substances as beverages and food. Human beings require protection from hazards—natural, supernatural and human—so culture offers housing and clothing, magic and medicine, army and police. Human beings require channels for the legitimate expression of their sexual impulses, so culture prescribes rules for mating and marriage. Human beings require a social matrix in which to belong and thrive, and culture defines [group life]. Human beings require frequent opportunities for physical exercise, and culture offers work and play. Human beings require answers to their questions and the exercise of their minds, and culture offers them a worldview, a logic, a method of interpreting experience. Human beings require means for the expression of their aspirations for excellence, and culture offers them esthetic and other norms. Finally, human beings require a sense of relationship with the Universe, and culture offers religion.[21]

The idea of culture helps us to critically reflect on our own way of life in the process of comparing it to others. By directly observing others about whom they knew little or nothing at all, anthropologists developed a notion of culture that has produced a richer understanding of human life and contributed to acknowledgment that all people experience time, space, and ultimate reality in a cultural context. If you are from Texas or El Salvador; if your parents are Native American, Euro-American, Asian American, Hispanic American, or African American; if you are Jewish, Catholic, Mormon, Amish, Methodist, Muslim, Hindu, Buddhist, Sikh, Taoist, Shintoist, or Santero; if you married the girl next door or your kids play with the gay couple's children up the street, culture is the basis of your interpretation of experience and generation of behavior.[22]

Members of local congregations can enlist anthropological tools to more effectively organize their evangelism in changing racial and ethnic contexts that require active transformation of institutional religious life. This is altogether important in a society where there is a strong desire for mainline churches to contribute to the formation of harmonious communities exclusive of separations determined by race, ethnicity, class, and gender. Cross-cultural approaches to evangelism promote among mainline Christians the commitment to explore with greater depth what makes human beings different and what constitutes their common humanity. Mainline Christians who pursue cross-cultural relationships and seriously work at reading life from the margins unfold a new way of looking at the world and model the kind of action that contributes to a shared sense of responsibility to global society.

As a boy, I was taken by the expectation God has for us to enter into cross-cultural relationship one afternoon in a South Bronx alleyway. I longed for a little money, and so I went into the alley behind a building on Westchester Avenue that was lined with about twenty garbage cans, a kid's gold mine. As a kid, I often rummaged through garbage cans to collect bottles that I took to the store in exchange for money. The familiar alleyway was different that morning owing to the unexpected presence of an old Jewish violinist, who showed me that the South Bronx also belonged to a wider world. He wore a dark blue wrinkled suit, a dress shirt more yellow than white, and a gray vest with a dangling gold watch chain. I had seen the old man in front of a store-front synagogue in the neighborhood, but never in an alley.

I stopped looking for bottles and listened to the old man's music, which was completely new to me. The old Jewish musician smiled at me and continued playing with closed eyes and slight up-and-down head movements. Windows on both sides of the alley began to open, and curious people leaned out of them. I saw Puerto Rican, Jewish, Italian, and Irish faces beaming into the alley. After each song, people threw coins and paper money wrapped in bathroom paper or scraps of the *Daily News* or *El diario la prensa*. I learned in a brief conversation with this man about Nazi death squads and camps where some members of his family had been killed. The numbers tattooed on his forearm were a constant reminder to him of the execution of millions at the hands of those who had the power to impose their vision of the world.

This old Jewish musician who played to a cross-cultural and interreligious crowd in a South Bronx alley knew firsthand the destructive capacity of mixing religion, racism, and nationalism. He tried that day to promote in me a desire for unity despite the contrast in our experiences. From a chance encounter I learned that the God who is qualitatively different from human beings shifts the terms of human relationships from hate and division to community and love. In a world where cultural differences give rise to seemingly irresolvable social conflicts, God takes the first step to overcome our divisions; indeed, God in Christ ensures our fundamental unity.

The alleyways of contemporary society indicate that mainline congregations concerned about evangelism need to be intentional about crossing cultural boundaries. In my view, the church acquires its deepest meaning when it finds God on the terrain of our differences. Members of congregations that embrace cultural others willingly move into a larger social landscape that reminds them that an authentic sense of life comes when there is recognition that history is already mixed with various and unique culture experiences. Evangelistic strategies that look at social reality from the perspective of the knowledge of members of another culture, their experience and articulation of major events, their lifestyles and material-cultural production (e.g., music, art, literature) is a way to overcome tribe-serving impulses that sidetrack the call to live for the well-being of others. Interestingly, the religion found in cyberspace is already fostering a cross-cultural understanding that has the potential to contribute to overcoming barriers of difference. Indeed, cyberspace religion "widens the social foundation of religious life . . . [and] erodes the basis from which religion contributes to the destructive dynamics of xenophobia."[23]

Below is a list of questions that will assist evangelistic approaches by deepening a congregation's understanding of the social and religious experience of other cultural groups. I suggest that in the process of recording responses to these questions, groups listen to the assumptions embedded in the answers regarding self and group identity, religious life, social relations, and ethnic changes in local communities. The questions below can be used for establishing relationships with other racial, ethnic, and cultural groups in local or global contexts.

Economic Life

What is your religious perspective on economic life?

What does the economy do *for* people and what does it do *to* them?

From your cultural viewpoint does national economic life produce social solidarity or social conflict?

How do you view the relationship between the local economy and the global economy?

What cultural factors guide the economic decisions you make each day?

What cultural factors might need to be considered to find solutions to problems in economic life in your community?

Are there identifiable links between social class and religious identity in your context?

What should economic life focus on?

What does it mean to be working poor, a consumer, unemployed, undocumented, a working woman?

What are the moral dimensions of economic life, and how do they relate to religious institutions?

What happens in Christian community when the God of life is separated from economic issues?

Social Life

What are the patterns of social relationships and the demographic characteristics in your community?

Who lives in the community now?

Do people relate to each other in terms of race, class, ethnicity, age group, sexual orientation, and so forth?

What is the basis for inclusion/exclusion in social groups?

What are the dominant social problems?

What other cultural knowledge systems compete with religion to address human needs and hopes for social life?

What general outlook on life is held by your cultural community?

How has your local church been altered by social change in the surrounding community?

Cultural Life

What are the predominant values of your cultural group?

What ideas reflect the consistent pattern of thought and behavior in your social group?

Are the cultural modes of action and the roles of cultural actors religiously motivated?

Who influences the system of meaning out of which people live?

What cultural knowledge are people using to generate behavior in their environment and to organize a meaningful self-identity?

How did you come to reside in your current community?

What is the nature of your experience in schools and with other ethnic groups?

Political Life

What is the relationship between political life and the system of beliefs constitutive of local culture?

How do people relate culture to their experience of politics?

What is the nature of political leadership?

Who has a voice and decision making power?

What role does religion, the media, and/or popular culture have on political life?

Whom do you think are the most exemplary leaders in your community, church, and society?

Religious Life

What is the religious climate of your local community?

Are categories of thought and behavior in community life religious or secular?

How does religion give expression to a cultural group's ultimate concern?

What religious symbols, beliefs, and practices play a role in the construction of group behavior and self-identity?

What is the social location of local religious leadership?

Does the local church's evangelistic strategy encourage members to understand pluralism and act on the relationship between the reconciling message of the gospel and social, political, and economic issues?

What is the view of your church toward racial and ethnic diversity?

What role does the social experience of marginality play in the local church's
construction of theological identity?

What sacred forces are present in local history and community experience?

When is/was religion most important in your life and that of members of your
local community?

Amid today's separating practices and withering faith witness, evangelism
means embodying a more active stance by valuing other cultures, respecting
them, and addressing the culturally defined needs of persons and groups. I
suggest that local congregations organize evangelism strategy groups to
engage in the formation of faith communities that promote cross-cultural
relationships for reconciling unity and civic engagement. For instance, an
evangelism strategy group can sponsor seminars, workshops, and leadership
training events to aid people in developing a more refined understanding of
culture, social interaction, and public life. Because culture serves as a foundational influence for human relationships, the mission of the evangelism strategy group is to guide the internal concerns of church members who seek to
share the good news of the gospel based on a substantive understanding of the
category of difference in society. By going out to meet the cultural other in the
world, members of local congregations develop a cross-cultural sensitivity to
the meaning of evangelism, see themselves from a new perspective, and appre-
hend anew the presence of God.

UNIVERSAL ASPECTS OF CULTURE

As I think back on my intercultural dialogue with the old Jewish violinist, I
realize today that it helped me recognize that a number of useful questions can
be raised in plural settings: If human beings have developed thousands of different cultures, how can we understand each other? If we perceive, feel, act,
and believe according to a specific cultural logic, are there identifiable universal characteristics of culture that form a basis for human unity? As an anthropologist, I recognize the existence of a number of cultural universals that I will
outline below to help evangelism groups in local congregations understand
what is similar about human beings.[24]

1. *Culture is learned, not genetically programmed.* The behavioral repertoire
of human beings is not genetically coded. Through a process of learning and

social interaction with one's environment, human beings acquire a cultural identity. Ideas, values, and behavior patterns are not innate characteristics; rather, human beings grow up in them. Because human behavior is not the product of genetics or instinct, it is amenable to change.

2. *Culture is shared by a group.* The shared beliefs and behavior patterns that are carried by members of a group in their heads organize every aspect of human experience to make life less complicated and to provide a sense of order and a certain level of predictability concerning how others will think and act. This dimension of culture is evidenced in children who through language, symbols, and behavior are socialized into their nation, religion, and ethnic identity.

3. *Culture is an adaptational mechanism.* This cultural characteristic is closely linked to learning, and it is responsible for enabling people to survive and thrive in diverse social and physical environments. Cultural inventions such as tools and technology, for instance, have helped human beings adapt to physical environments once thought unsuitable for habitation, such as deserts, polar regions, oceans, and outer space.

4. *Culture is normative.* Every social group has written and unwritten rules for cultural interaction. For instance, norms specify what is appropriate and inappropriate conduct in social situations, such as "Wash your hands before eating," "Keep your shoes off the table," or the idea in American society that women must remove facial and body hair. Generally, culture demands conformity, rejects deviance, and serves to support the existing way of life and prevailing system of power and prestige.

These four cultural universals focus attention on material, ideational, and behavioral aspects of culture. Through a process of learning from generation to generation, members of specific social groups acquire the cultural knowledge that assigns meaning to things, interprets experience, and generates behavior in the physical and social environment. These universals tend to center attention on aspects of cultural continuity and the more static features of a cultural system, but culture is always undergoing change either from internal innovation or external intervention. The following three universals are more dynamic.

5. *Culture is heterogeneous.* A dynamic feature of culture that is particularly noticeable in multicultural societies like the United States is that a shared cultural identity can be experienced differently. Being American, for instance, may translate into an evaluation of social reality differently by virtue of ethnicity, class, sexual orientation, gender, racial identity, and linguistic preference. Within the Christian community, one sees this cultural variance in theological identity. For instance, Christians in Asia, Latin America, and Africa look to their churches to find solutions to desperate problems of eco-

nomic exploitation and human rights violations. Members of the mainstream culture in the United States, however, tend to harmonize their beliefs with existing systems of oppression and ideologies of power.

6. *Culture is always changing.* Internal cultural change can be brought about by interactive shifts in a society's technological, ideological, environmental, and social relationships. Additionally, cultural change is often initiated by processes of cultural diffusion or borrowing, which was noted by the anthropologist Ralph Linton with respect to culture in the United States:

> Our solid American citizen awakens in a bed built on a pattern which originated in the Near East but which was modified in northern Europe before it was transmitted to America. He throws back covers made from cotton, domesticated in India, or linen, domesticated in the Near East, or wool from sheep, also domesticated in the Near East, or silk, the use of which was discovered in China. All of these materials have been spun and woven by processes invented in the Near East. He slips into moccasins, invented by the Indians of the Eastern Woodlands, and goes to the bathroom, whose fixtures are a mixture of European and American inventions, both of recent date. He takes off his pajamas, a garment invented in India, and washes with soap invented by the ancient Gauls. . . . He reads the news of the day, imprinted in characters invented by the ancient Semites upon a material invented in China by a process invented in Germany. As he absorbs the accounts of foreign troubles he will, if he is a good conservative citizen, thank a Hebrew deity in an Indo-European language that he is 100 percent American.[25]

7. *Culture is arbitrary.* Meaning is attached by cultural actors to people and things in accordance with the categories of thought specific to a cultural community. Every culture divides up the world with the help of cultural ideas that mediate to members of a social group a sense of the way things "really are." Although cultural categories organize every aspect of human experience, the ones selected and used are nonetheless arbitrary. For instance, an American socialized into the dominant culture would agree that a table is a piece of furniture consisting of a flat, horizontal top typically set on legs. This person would not call this piece of furniture a chair, which is defined as a piece of furniture for one person to sit on that is generally set on four legs. What one should remember is that the cultural ideas of chair and table are arbitrary designations consistently used over time. The cultural system of ideas could have encompassed the objects of furniture differently by teaching people to call a chair a table, and a table a chair.

Evangelistic approaches that guide congregations on the journey to become an intentionally diverse community will find that using the plan outlined above for developing cross-cultural competence will contribute to sensibilities that promote respect for persons who live with different worldviews, value systems, beliefs, and behaviors. In a postmodern world threatened by fragmentation, violence, nihilism, and meaninglessness, effective communication of the power of the gospel means taking the basic message that in Christ the world has changed across cultural boundaries so that those who already believe may find their deepest human identity—namely, as people of hope in a future world transformed by a generous and welcoming God that is known by strangers when breaking bread (Luke 24:35). In our post–September 11 world, we need to proclaim that we receive God's gift of peace not by overcoming a divided world with destructive hate, but by embracing it with reconciliation and forgiveness.

Because Jesus spent his time challenging the cultural practices and rules that maintained exclusive boundaries between different communities—men and women, adults and children, rich and poor, healthy and sick, chosen and rejected, Jews and others—evangelism today must not overlook the importance of accepting differences and creating unity in the world. Evangelism is more than talk about God's good news; instead, it means listening to cultural others long enough to be changed by their words, struggles, longings, and vulnerabilities in order to understand the One who came "not to be served, but to serve, and to give his life a ransom for many" (Mark 10:45). The mainline Christian church finds its identity when the generosity of God revealed by Jesus to his first hearers transforms it into a community of inclusive compassion.[26]

JESUS MEETS OTHERS

From the perspective of the barrio, scriptural interpretation in the local congregation should help members see the incredible world of languages, ethnicities, nationalities, and religious groups that constituted the early Christian world.[27] The hermeneutics of diversity makes plain how various social locations influenced the production of Christian writings. For instance, Mark is written from the perspective of rural peasants, Luke expresses a commitment to the poor, Matthew writes as an educated Jewish urbanite, John reflects the situation of marginalized Jews in Ephesus, and Paul writes to a variety of groups in the Mediterranean world.[28] In part, the Scriptures suggest that the structure of theological identity is distorted when the historical experiences of different social groups that shaped the message of the New Testament writers are ignored.

The New Testament includes stories of Jesus announcing the good news of God's reign to persons from other cultures and turning the world upside down

STOP

I sent for you
because the thousand
excuses you make on

the other side of
this wall keep the
infant twins in the

Rivera apartment you
never visit in front
of a television set

dying of AIDS while
Mister Rogers sings
it's a beautiful day

in the neighborhood.
I sent for the police
chief who wants to lock

up their junkie parents,
the politicians who want
votes, the "putas" who

walk your side of the
wall with married men
who want to be happy,

the religious leaders
who pray for you to forget
the questions junkies, whores,

and dead kids ask. I sent
for all of you because so
much talk of changing the

world on your side
of the wall is cheap
now and at the hour

of our death.

by opposing the status quo. The kingdom of God announced by Jesus removed religious and social barriers that prevented human beings from grasping the reality of God's will for inclusive community. Jesus called on his followers to establish new relationships not based on discriminatory practices or relationally limited ideologies. He tore down oppositional walls to create community between the rich and poor, the educated and uneducated, Jews and foreigners, rural peasants and urban elites, the healthy and the sick, the righteous and sinners. He also sided with groups denied equality in society, such as the poor, the sick, tax collectors, mourners, prostitutes, women, and children.[29] In short, Jesus revealed the God who loves the vast array of human beings in the world and restores their dignity and righteousness.[30]

The story of Jesus and the Samaritan woman in John 4 suggests that God breaks into our lives through relationships that cross the boundaries that keep people apart (Mark 1:40–45; 5:25–34; 7:24–30). We learn from this story that living in Christian community involves crossing into forbidden territory to be in relationship with racially rejected and unwelcome people. Jesus was traveling with his disciples through the region of Samaria known for its association with Jacob, an impressive ancestor of the Hebrew people.[31] Because the story begins with the statement "Now he had to go through Samaria" (John 4:4), the reader is immediately left asking a number of questions: Why would a group of people who were culturally opposed to the Samaritans travel through Samaria? Did it make the trip back to Galilee quicker or safer for Jesus and his disciples?

The evangelist tells us that Jesus passed through the Samaritan city of Sychar and stopped by Jacob's well. Jesus' lengthy conversation with the Samaritan woman touches on such themes as biological need, ethnicity, relationships, and religious traditions. For some commentators the time of day chosen by the woman for drawing water suggests the woman has loose morals. But the story does not really tell us she is of questionable moral character, only that she married two times more than permitted by Jewish law and was now living with a man (4:18). Nothing in the text leads us to conclude the Samaritan woman is ethically disordered; additionally, Jesus does not urge the woman to change her lifestyle or ask forgiveness for past behavior. The story seems simply to illustrate the Great Commission as God's concern to break barriers to cross-cultural relationship.[32]

Jesus' unfolding relationship with the Samaritan woman proposes that partnership with God is not limited by place, gender, ethnicity, religion, or worldview. As the conversation begins, the woman tells Jesus that ethnicity is a barrier to their full human relationship: "How is it that you, a Jew, ask a drink of me, a woman of Samaria?" (4:9). Jesus should not be talking to this woman or sharing her drinking utensils, because in the view of established Judaism the Samaritans were viewed as religiously and ethnically inferior. The nameless Samaritan woman, who knew the meaning of lesser status in society, at first only perceives a Jewish man asking her for water. In other words, her encounter is alienated by a dehumanizing ideology of ethnic antagonism and gender expectations.[33]

In the ancient Near East, wells were a good place to meet women who came to draw household water. But a well was hardly a place for an extraordinary encounter, especially with a person like Jesus who defined reality without imposing rules of separation. That the Samaritan woman reminds Jesus of their ethnic differences shows her captivity to a web of cultural beliefs and behavior that impedes positive intercultural relationships. Yet Jesus knows the woman will find her greatest depth by moving away from her conventional understanding of the order of life and its religious conceptions, which count on God to maintain ethnic and gender divisions. The woman first misunderstands what Jesus is saying to her about living water, since she cannot imagine Jesus offering any better water than that found in the well (4:10–12). But Jesus goes on to clarify for her that he offers "a spring of water gushing up to eternal life" (4:14).

Jesus' behavior toward the Samaritan woman demonstrates the nonexclusive love of God for human beings. He rejects the normative understanding that contamination would come to him by way of contact with the woman, and he becomes an active agent of the God who only demands love. The woman discovers by the well that by living in compassionate relationship to others exclusive of any kind of alienation, the life-denying consequences of ethnic division are obliterated. Jesus reveals the God who aims to save us from a world that holds some people down and lifts others up. Although the personal, cultural, and theological expectations of the Samaritan woman are conditioned by the messy business of life, they are altered by her encounter with Jesus. The message of Jesus enables her to let go of alienating ideas in order to embrace a new way of living in the world: "Sir, give me this water, so that I may never be thirsty or have to keep coming here to draw water" (4:15).

What I find most inviting about this story is the suggestion that Jesus invites us to live beyond the present order of ethnic and gender relationships and its structure of self-interest by embracing our differences as a sign of the God who is always more than what we think. This story tells us that the barriers that make life less whole and prevent reconciliation between opposed groups are traversed first by Jesus. The disciples who are agitated over Jesus' conversation with the foreign woman fail to understand that the barrier-breaking

Jesus is already modeling salvation by entering into relationship with one defined as unclean by mainline religion (4:27).[34] The Samaritan woman gradually recognizes that Jesus is the living water who satisfies life, the one who declares all things to us (4:25), and the one who creates community through diversity.[35]

By a common well, Jesus and a Samaritan woman entered into a relationship that overturned the conventional religious and cultural expectations. The experience of Jesus overcoming cultures of separation produces a thirst for the "living water" that issues forth in a new understanding of God and that makes one a coworker in God's building project of hospitable community. The Samaritan woman, liberated from the limitations imposed on her by culture, claims her voice to speak to others of a reconciling God. Once she was a social nobody rejected by the adherents of orthodox Judaism and looked down upon by members of her own community, but after meeting Jesus she becomes an evangelist in her world where women are counted as inferior. She goes back to her people to live differently in the world and is focused on sharing the good news of God's gracious gift to all people.

The story of Jesus and the Samaritan woman speaks to the church about a God who is religiously critical, culturally transforming, and radically welcoming. As Judith Gundry-Volf observes, the story suggests that "believing in Jesus is also at the same reconciliation between those who are estranged, the creation of an inclusive fellowship."[36] One doesn't have to look very far in congregational life to find persons who have grown careless and cynical about faith in God's diverse creation and who hang onto their culture of separation. Class, education, race, ethnicity, immigration status, gender, age, language, and sexual orientation are some of the walls that divide people inside and outside of the church. Yet the mark of genuine Christian community is the commitment to overcome distrust and misunderstanding by surrendering to the foolishness of love and walking with Jesus Christ in the generosity of fellowship that points toward God's reign.

In our global society, the church cannot afford to create life together on the principles of exclusion, but should instead strive for that fellowship of love in which there are no outcasts, strangers, and racial aliens, but "citizens with the saints and also members of the household of God" (Eph. 2:19).[37] The church's commitment to diversity requires finding God not in systems of domination over others, but through the grace of a life-giving God who works through cultures to address human needs and who is always close to suffering people. Today the commitment to justice and reconciliation means opening the local church to the vast variety of human beings who are valued by God and placed in our way to love.

CONCLUSION

Local congregations whose members seriously relate the good news of the gospel to cultural diversity are in the position to more deeply pursue evangelism that helps build a world of tolerance and solidarity. In our global society, one sure way for Christians to overcome the denial of others is to increase their interaction, communication, and cooperation with people who hold different cultural identities, worldviews, religious practices, values, and languages. As we look to the future, the anthropological concepts and field approaches discussed above for use in evangelism projects will foster a deeper understanding of the meaning of diversity and what cultural identity tells us about the religious and intellectual ordering of life. In short, church practices that welcome strangers into community life today should call persons to see themselves anew and act contrary to the conventions of a divided world.

What we are facing today in evangelism is the challenge of creating diverse mainline congregations based on the understanding that God created human beings to express a multiplicity of languages, lifestyles, and ways of thinking and acting in the world. For God the world is not divided, and God's people are to be a foretaste of the unity envisioned by God's love in Christ. By intentionally understanding and welcoming people of different cultural backgrounds into the local church, Christians undergo the transformation necessary to proclaim the gospel of a community-commanding God. In short, as the local congregation becomes diverse by engaging in cross-cultural evangelism and relationships, it will embody a gospel that is open to the reality of the universal promises of God's reign.

In our time of major social change and of theological engagement with the complexities of polarizing racial and ethnic ideologies,[38] mainline churches can learn from Jesus' encounter with the Samaritan woman to listen to the racially despised and people pushed aside by society. The freedom for which Christ sets us free establishes the basic conditions for the mainline church to face the challenges before it and to unfold new relationships across racial, ethnic, and cultural communities. As the mainline church turns to the barrio to find the sources of its institutional renewal, it will find the new resources with which to courageously proclaim a message of radical trust in the Christ who reveals life's deepest meaning and who says to love those whom God never turns away.

Notes

Introduction

1. Bureau of the Census, Current Population Reports, "National Population Projections Resident Population of the United States: Middle Series Projections, 2035–2050, by Sex, Race, and Hispanic Origin, with Median Age" (Washington, DC, 1996).
2. See Joe Feagan, "Old Poison in New Bottles: The Deep Roots of Modern Nativism," *Immigrants Out!*, ed. Juan Perea (New York: New York University Press, 1997), 13.

Chapter 1: Walk with Christ from the Color Line to the Borderline

1. Many mainline churches are struggling with additional crisis issues, such as their stance on homosexuality, biblical interpretation and authority, understanding of mission, interreligious relationships, women's reproductive rights, and spiritual relativism.
2. In *Man's Most Dangerous Myth* (1974), Ashley Montagu says that the idea of race has resulted in the production of white humanity's most dangerous and tragic myth (idea of white superiority) that constructs attitudes, practices, and worldviews resulting in the death, disempowerment, and brutalization of millions of human beings considered inferior.
3. Although Latinos are ethnic Americans who can be viewed in terms of particular national groups with characteristic cultural traits or social practices, the racism in mainstream American society racially constructs their identity and designates them "persons of color." Although Latinos can represent any number of racial groups, even so-called white Hispanics who find themselves on the lower economic scale, speak with an accent, and have low levels of education are negatively racialized as well.
4. Black theologian James Cone is angry about the silence of white theologians on the question of racism and how the myth of white supremacy contradicts Christian belief. It is no less infuriating for Native Americans, Latinos, and Asians to be written out of the history of the oppressed in America by most black and white theologians and public intellectuals. See James H. Cone, *Risks*

of Faith: The Emergence of a Black Theology of Liberation, 1968–1998 (Boston: Beacon Press, 1999).

5. Charles Taylor, "The Politics of Recognition," in *Multiculturalism* (Princeton, NJ: Princeton University Press, 1994), 25.

6. Cornel West, *Race Matters* (Boston: Beacon Press, 1993), 2–3.

7. Regrettably, established scholars like Cornel West who have on occasion noted the need to move beyond biracial framing of the politics of race disregard the fact that Latinos have been lynched in the Southwest, beaten down by white and even black police officers (e.g., Daniel Gomez was shot in the back by a black police officer in Washington, DC, sparking an urban riot in 1992), and been economically exploited, politically repressed, and culturally raped. Scholarship dealing with the politics of race in America needs to acknowledge that Native American contact with so-called white settlers resulted in near genocide, Puerto Rican contact resulted in colonial subordination and cultural rape, and Chicano contacts in the Southwest led to conquest. Japanese Americans experienced hostility that included one of the greatest civil rights violations of the twentieth century, which came with their relocation to concentration camps during World War II. That West makes race matter only in black and white serves to confirm the dominant myths about who legitimately belongs in American society.

8. The growth of the Latino community has caught the attention of Harvard professor Samuel Huntington. In his *Who Are We? The Challenges to America's National Identity* (New York: Simon & Schuster, 2004), he engages in Latino-phobic reasoning to whip up hysteria about how Latinos who he claims do not assimilate threaten Anglo-Protestant culture. The idea that the United States is a society offering freedom to the oppressed and persons seeking a better life is hardly recalled in the pages of this new book. Instead, the moralistic tone of the work, its nostalgia for Anglo-Protestant culture and attack on Latinos who helped build the nation and continue to contribute to its strength sadly recommend it as a contemporary text in racist scholarship.

9. Frank Bonilla, "Changing the Americas from within the United States," in *Borderless Borders: U.S. Latinos, Latin Americans, and the Paradox of Interdependence*, ed. Frank Bonilla et al. (Philadelphia: Temple University Press, 1998), x–xi.

10. U.S. Department of Education, "School Dropout Prevention Program," http://www.ed.gov/programs/dropout/index.html.

11. In *Mañana: Christian Theology from a Hispanic Perspective* (Nashville: Abingdon Press, 1990), Justo L. González says that not only are Anglo-Americans newcomers to this land compared to Hispanics, but the dominant culture must come to terms with the history of injustice at the heart of its power and social order.

12. For a work that focuses on the way religion shapes and maintains racial and ethnic identity, see Craig R. Prentiss, ed., *Religion and the Creation of Race and Ethnicity* (New York: New York University Press, 2003).

13. Howard Winant, *The World Is a Ghetto: Race and Democracy since World War II* (New York: Basic Books, 2001), 1

14. Howard Winant, "Racism Today: Continuity and Change in the Post-Civil Rights Era," in *Race, Ethnicity, and Nationality in the United States*, ed. Paul Wong (Boulder, CO: Westview Press, 1999), 22.

15. Winant, *World Is a Ghetto*, 1.

16. Ibid., 38.

17. Ibid., 24–25.

18. See Ruth Benedict, *Race and Racism* (London: Routledge, 1942), 97.

19. Winant, *World Is a Ghetto*, 28.
20. See Emmanuel Chukwude Eze, ed., *Race and the Enlightenment: A Reader* (Cambridge: Blackwell, 1997); David Theo Goldber, *Racist Culture: Philosophy and the Politics of Meaning* (Cambridge: Blackwell, 1993); and Paul R. Griffin, *Seeds of Racism in the Soul of America* (Cleveland: Pilgrim Press, 1999).
21. Emmanuel Chukwude Eze, ed., *Race and the Enlightenment*, intro. and chap. 3.
22. See John Van Evrie, *White Supremacy and Negro Subordination* (1861; repr., New York: Negro Universities Press, 1969).
23. As quoted in Kathryn Shanley, "The Thinking Heart: American Indian Discourse and the Politics of Recognition," in Wong, *Race, Ethnicity, and Nationality in the United States*, 269.
24. Eduardo Bonilla-Silva, "The New Racism," in Wong, *Race, Ethnicity, and Nationality in the United States*, 57.
25. Martin Luther King Jr., "A Challenge to the Churches and Synagogues," in *Race: Challenge to Religion*, ed. Mathew Ahmann (Chicago: H. Regenery Co., 1963), 164.
26. As quoted in Henry Y. Ueno, *Manzanar Martyr* (Anaheim, CA: Shumway Family History Services, 1986), v.
27. For American Christians the racial divide should have been overcome when God accepted the marriage of Moses to a black woman (Num. 12:1) and at Pentecost where every race and nation heard in its own tongue of God's saving action (Acts 2:5–13); however, the quest for democracy in the United States has never been unburdened of the principles of racial exclusion.
28. Gilbert Paul Carrasco, "Latinos in the United States: Invitation and Exile," in *The Latino Condition: A Critical Reader*, ed. Richard Delgado and Jesan Stefancic (New York: New York University Press, 1998), 82.
29. Henry A. Giroux, "Living Dangerously: Identity Politics and the New Cultural Racism," in *Between Borders*, ed. Henry A. Giroux and Peter McLaren (New York: Routledge, 1994), 38.
30. See Samuel Huntington's nativist ravings in "The Hispanic Challenge," *Foreign Policy* 141 (March/April 2004). Huntington's is less a demonstration of reasoned scholarship than a display of anti-immigrant sentiment that negates the idea of American nationhood and shows ignorance with respect to American Latinos.
31. Thomas Muller, "Nativism in the Mid-1990s," in *Immigrants Out! The New Nativism and the Anti-Immigrant Impulse in the United States*, ed. Juan F. Perea (New York: New York University Press, 1997), 109.
32. Ian F. Haney Lopez, *White by Law: The Legal Construction of Race* (New York: New York University Press, 1996), 41–42.
33. In *The Presumed Alliance: The Unspoken Conflict between Latinos and Blacks and What It Means for America* (New York: HarperCollins, 2004), Nicolas Vaca presents a powerful analysis of the politics of race in American society focusing attention on black and Latino tensions and the need to move toward an enlarged civil and human rights framework. Indeed, he argues against the black-white analytical framework that has determined race relations and that scholars such as Cornel West and Angela Harris defend by insisting on the unique role of African Americans in American history. Vaca's enlarged reading of race relations in America holds that the future of American society will be "greatly influenced by Latinos and their culture" (202).
34. Alejandro Portes and Ruben G. Rumabaut, *Immigrant America: A Portrait* (Berkeley: University of California Press, 1990), 98–99.

35. Joe Feagan, "Old Poison in New Bottles: The Deep Roots of Modern Nativism," in Perea, *Immigrants Out!* 15.

36. See Matthew Frye Jacobson, *Whiteness of a Different Color: European Immigrants and the Alchemy of Race* (Cambridge, MA: Harvard University Press, 1998).

37. In *The Disuniting of America*, Schlesinger argues that ethnic studies threaten to decompose America. He is critical of scholarship emerging from communities of color that challenge the hegemonic discourse of white dominant liberal education (see chaps. 2–4).

38. Benjamin Ringer, in *"We the People" and Others: Duality and America's Treatment of Its Racial Minorities* (New York: Tavistock Publications, 1983), discusses pluralism in American society in light of racial and ethnic interaction and power struggles and how the founding legal documents promoted a racial divide and second-class citizenship.

39. See Georges Fauriol, ed., *Security in the Americas* (Washington, DC: National Defense University Press, 1989).

40. See Pedro Cabin, "The New Synthesis of Latin American and Latino Studies," in Bonilla et al., *Borderless Borders*, 196.

41. Vaca, *Presumed Alliance*, 188.

42. As quoted in Olga Briseno, "Mister Migra, Harold Ezzell," *San Diego Union-Tribune* (August 23, 1989): F1.

43. As quoted by Pedro Caban, "The New Synthesis of Latin American and Latino Studies," in Bonilla et al., *Borderless Borders*, 198.

44. Linda B. Hayes, "Letter to the Editor: California's Pro. 187," *New York Times*, October 15, 1994, 18.

45. Barbara Coe, "Keep Illegals Out of the State," *USA Today*, October, 12, 1994, 12A.

46. David Bacon, "Immigrants: Are Undocumented Workers Being Thrown to the Wolves?" http://www.igc.apc.org/dbacon/Imgrants/12split.html.

47. Roberto Suro, *Strangers among Us* (New York: Vintage Press, 1999), 114–15.

48. Peter Brimelow, *Alien Nation: Common Sense About America's Immigration Disaster* (New York: HarperPerennial, 1996), 56.

49. Raoul Lowery Contreras, "Racists Wish to Turn America as It Had Evolved in 1965," *El Hispano* (Sacramento, CA) (August 11, 1993): 3.

50. Brimelow, *Alien Nation*, 218. See also Huntington, *Who Are We?*

51. See Ronald Takaki, *A Different Mirror: A History of Multicultural America* (New York: Little, Brown & Co., 1993).

52. Daniel Kanstrom, "Dangerous Undertones of the New Nativism: Peter Brimelow and the Decline of the West," in Perea, *Immigrants Out!* 305.

53. See Alejandro Portes and Ruben G. Rumbaut, *Legacies: The Story of the Immigrant Second Generation* (Berkeley: University of California Press, 2001), 271–72.

54. Ibid., 271.

55. I am indebted to Jürgen Moltmann for this rich conceptual imagery about Christ offering life before death and a world that gives us death before life. See Moltmann, *The Open Church: Invitation to a Messianic Lifestyle* (Philadelphia: Fortress Press, 1978).

Chapter 2: Good News from the Barrio

1. On the idea of the centrality of the reign of God, initiation into Christian community, and a critique of church growth, see William Abraham, *The Logic of Evangelism* (Grand Rapids: Wm. B. Eerdmans Publishing Co., 1989).

2. Walter Brueggemann, *Biblical Perspectives on Evangelism* (Nashville: Abingdon Press, 1993), 44–45.
3. Ibid., 46.
4. See Brueggemann, *Biblical Perspectives on Evangelism*; and Craig M. Gay, *The Way of the (Modern) World, or, Why It's Tempting to Live as if God Doesn't Exist* (Grand Rapids: Wm. B. Eerdmans Publishing Co., 1998).
5. Gerald Anderson, cited in "Mission Evangelism: To Make Disciples," *New World Outlook*, May 1988, 9.
6. Evangelization means proclaiming with words and Christian action the ongoing presence of Jesus Christ in the affairs of human beings. This fundamental presence of Christ among us converts the baptized today to the liberative activity of God in the world and directs the church in service of the world.
7. See Orlando Costas, *Christ outside the Gate* (Maryknoll, NY: Orbis Books, 1984), chap. 10.
8. Orlando Costas, *Liberating News: A Theology of Contextual Evangelization* (Grand Rapids: Wm. B. Eerdmans Publishing Co., 1989), 62.
9. See Jürgen Moltmann, *The Open Church: Invitation to a Messianic Lifestyle* (Philadelphia: Fortress Press, 1978), 105.
10. Ibid., chap. 14.
11. Jack Nelson-Pallmeyer, *Jesus against Christianity: Reclaiming the Missing Jesus* (Harrisburg, PA: Trinity Press International, 2003), ix.
12. John Dominic Crossan, *The Birth of Christianity: Discovering What Happened in the Years Immediately after the Execution of Jesus* (San Francisco: HarperSanFrancisco, 1998), xxx.
13. Walter Brueggemann, *The Prophetic Imagination* (Philadelphia: Fortress Press, 1978), 13.
14. Ibid. See also Martin Buber, *The Prophetic Faith* (New York: Harper & Brothers, 1949), 2–3.
15. Mary C. Grey, *The Outrageous Pursuit of Hope: Prophetic Dreams for the Twenty-First Century* (London: Darton, Longman & Todd, 2000), 13.
16. See Gustavo Gutierrez, *The God of Life* (Maryknoll, NY: Orbis Books, 1991), chap. 5.
17. James M. Ward, *The Prophets* (Nashville: Abingdon Press, 1982), 143.
18. Gustavo Gutierrez, *A Theology of Liberation* (Maryknoll, NY: Orbis Books, 1971), 293.
19. See John W. De Gruchy, *Christianity and Democracy: A Theology of a Just World Order* (Cambridge: Cambridge University Press, 1995).
20. See John E. Tropman, *Does America Hate the Poor? The Other American Dilemma: Lessons for the 21st Century from the 1960s and the 1970s* (Westport, CT: Praeger Publications, 1998).
21. U.S. Census Bureau, *Poverty Thresholds 2003*, http://www.census.gov/hhes/poverty/threshld/thresh03.html.
22. Children's Defense Fund, "Defining Poverty and Why It Matters for Children" (Washington, D.C., Aug. 2004), 2, http://www.childrendefense.org/familyincome/childpoverty/definingpoverty.pdf.
23. Three out of the ten poorest counties in the United States are found in the borderlands. Compared with the rest of the country, the unemployment rate is 250–300 percent higher in these communities.
24. U.S. Department of Housing and Urban Development, "Facts about Farmworkers and Colonias," http://www.hud.gov/groups/farmwkercolonia.cfm.

25. Anup Shah, "Poverty Facts and Stats," http://www.globalissues.org/TradeRe-lated/Facts.asp.

26. Salih Booker and William Minter, "Global Apartheid," *The Nation* (July 9, 2001), http://www.thenation.com/doc/20010709/booker.

27. Human Development Report 2000, *United Nations Development Programme* (NY: United Nations Publication, 2000), 82.

28. John Cavanagh and Sarah Anderson, "World Billionaires Take a Hit, but Still Soar," *Institute for Policy Studies*, March 6, 2002, http://www.ips-dc.org/.

29. See Joseph Stiglitz, *Globalization and Its Discontents* (New York: W. W. Norton & Co., 2002).

30. See Eleanor Leacock, "Distortions of Working-Class Reality in American Social Science," *Science and Society* 31 (1967): 3–4.

31. This is precisely what took place when *Time* ran an article on the poor titled, "The American Underclass: Destitute and Desperate in a Land of Plenty," 110, no. 9 (August 29, 1977). The cover featured black and Hispanic faces, male and female, appearing defeated in their poverty and isolated from mainstream society. The so-called underclass living within the crumbling walls of the slums were socially alienated from the rest of society and even unreachable due to values unlike those shared by the wider society. The looting during the July 1977 blackout in New York City was blamed on the underclass, whose suffering at the margins of society commanded no attention by those quick to criminalize them for being poor.

32. In his *The Working Poor* (New York: Alfred A. Knopf, 2004), David K. Shipler uses this phrase to discuss how Harrington's work raised awareness in U.S. society to the plight of the poor. However, Shipler also notes that forty years after the publication of Harrington's book the gap between the top 10 percent of Americans (median net worth of $833,600) and the bottom 20 percent (median net worth of $7,900) has grown even worse.

33. Michael Harrington, *The Other America* (New York: Macmillan, 1962), 191.

34. As quoted in Michael Katz, *The Undeserving Poor: From the War on Poverty to the War on Welfare* (New York: Pantheon Books, 1989), 24.

35. See Katz, *Undeserving Poor*, chap. 2.

36. By this I mean the coming together within and across cultural boundaries for a common purpose.

37. Herbert J. Gans, *The War against the Poor* (New York: Basic Books, 1995), 66.

38. See Valerie Polakow, *Lives on the Edge: Single Mothers and Their Children in the Other America* (Chicago: University of Chicago Press, 1993).

39. See Katz, *Undeserving Poor*, 185.

40. Gans, *War against the Poor*, 59.

41. Ibid., 85.

42. See Marian Wright Edelman, *Families in Peril: An Agenda for Social Change* (Cambridge, MA: Harvard University Press, 1987).

43. See Tropman, *Does America Hate the Poor?*

44. Gutierrez, *Theology of Liberation*, 291–92. See also Waldron Scott, *Bring Forth Justice* (Grand Rapids: Wm. B. Eerdmans Publishing Co., 1980), 150–51; and Clodovis Boff and George Pixley, *The Bible, the Church, and the Poor* (Mary-knoll, NY: Orbis Books, 1986).

45. In *Jesus: A Revolutionary Biography* (San Francisco: HarperSanFrancisco, 1994), John Dominic Crossan explains that the blessing extended by Jesus to the poor was not to the general peasant class, but specifically to the destitute or those

persons squeezed out of life by the oppressive practices of the dominant social system.

46. José Cárdenas Pallares, *A Poor Man Called Jesus: Reflections on the Gospel of Mark* (Maryknoll, NY: Orbis Books, 1990), 45.
47. Boff and Pixley, *Bible, the Church, and the Poor,* 111.
48. See Pallares, *Poor Man Called Jesus,* 6–8.
49. Ched Meyers, *Binding the Strong Man: A Political Reading of Mark's Story of Jesus* (Maryknoll, NY: Orbis Books, 1988), 156.
50. See David Tracy, "The Hidden God: The Divine Other of Liberation," *Cross Currents* 46, no. 1 (Spring 1996): 5–12. I am indebted to Tracy for his discussion of God entering history in hiddenness, in the encounter with the suffering other of history, in liberating forms of contemporary theology articulated by the weak and voiceless, and as the other who interrupts the experience and narratives of dominant culture.
51. Joachim Jeremias, *The Parables of Jesus* (New York: Charles Scribner's Sons, 1954), 122.
52. Today the movement of women into the sex trade is induced by poverty, lack of opportunities, the low status of women in various cultures, and an international organized crime network for which the sex trade generates between five and seven billion dollars annually. The good news of Christ announced by the church finds its bearings when the church recognizes God disclosed in persons whose existence is threatened by formal and informal economies of consumption that severely damage the least of God's children. See Joanna Kerr and Caroline Sweetman, *Women Reinventing Globalization* (Oxford, Oxfam: 2003), 125.
53. Phyllis A. Bird, "Images of Women in the Old Testament," in *The Bible and Liberation,* ed. Norman K. Gottwald (Maryknoll, NY: Orbis Books, 1983), 272.
54. Jeremias, *Parables of Jesus,* 127.
55. Craig L. Bloomberg, *Interpreting the Parables* (Downers Grove, IL: InterVarsity Press, 1990), 186.
56. Jeremias, *Parables of Jesus,* 127.
57. Jürgen Moltmann, *The Way of Jesus Christ* (Minneapolis: Fortress Press, 1993), 101.

Chapter 3: They Go to the Altar

1. Robert McAfee Brown, *Spirituality of Liberation: Overcoming the Great Fallacy* (Philadelphia: Westminster Press, 1988), 116.
2. See Jon Sobrino, *Christology at the Crossroads* (Maryknoll, NY: Orbis Books, 1978); and Gustavo Gutierrez, *We Drink from Our Own Wells: The Spiritual Journey of a People* (Maryknoll, NY: Orbis Books, 1998).
3. Sociologists identify a basic shift in spirituality these days that reflects little inclination to subscribe to rigid belief systems and a clear preference for a kind of free market spirituality.
4. See Robert Wuthnow, *After Heaven: Spirituality in America since the 1950s* (Berkeley: University of California Press, 1998); Wade Clark Roof, *Spiritual Marketplace: Baby Boomers and the Remaking of American Religion* (Princeton, NJ: Princeton University Press, 1999).
5. See Marcus J. Borg, *Meeting Jesus Again for the First Time* (San Francisco: HarperSanFranciso, 1994). Borg's discussion of contemporary Jesus scholarship directs attention to the quest to find a mature faith in the context of Christian tradition. While Borg invites readers to find a meaningful image of Jesus,

especially by understanding and embracing a relationship with the living Christ, I suggest that Jesus is waiting to renew the spiritual life of mainline Christians in the barrio where God affirms and sacralizes the world of trampled human beings.

6. See Wuthnow, *After Heaven*; and Roof, *Spiritual Marketplace*.

7. See Eric Michael Mazur and Kate McCarthy, eds., *God in the Details: American Religion in Popular Culture* (New York: Routledge, 2001).

8. Wuthnow, *After Heaven*, 3–4.

9. Ibid., 40.

10. See Wuthnow, *After Heaven*, chap. 2.

11. Wuthnow, *After Heaven*, 8.

12. Ibid., 57.

13. At the time dwelling spirituality was strong, third-world theologians were quite critical of the cultural captivity of American Christianity that harmonized God with nationalism, racism, classism, authoritarianism, or debates about who possessed the truth on matters of faith.

14. See Z. Bauman, "Postmodern Religion," in *Religion, Modernity, and Post-Modernity*, ed. P. Heelas (Oxford: Blackwell, 1992); and J. Lyotard, *The Post-Modern Condition* (Manchester: Manchester University Press, 1984).

15. Liberal Protestant forces held the position of dominance in spiritual and political matters in American culture since the trial of John Scopes (the biology teacher who defied Tennessee's anti-evolution law in 1925) until the 1970s. Authors such as Sinclair Lewis, whose Elmer Gantry figure epitomized the liberal and educated classes' view of the fundamentalist preacher (hypocrite, swindler, and bigot), and H. L. Mencken, who covered the Scopes trial and thought fundamentalist beliefs represented a type of "malignant imbecility," reinforced negative assessments of fundamentalism in the wider culture. If fundamentalist Christians went into exile following the Scopes trial, they entered the public square with stunning force in the 1980s.

16. See Susan Harding, *The Book of Jerry Falwell* (Princeton, NJ: Princeton University Press, 2000).

17. Wuthnow, *After Heaven*, 107.

18. Ibid., 113.

19. See James Davison Hunter, *Evangelicalism: The Coming Generation* (Chicago: Chicago University Press, 1987).

20. Roof, *Spiritual Marketplace*, 297.

21. See Susan Field Harding, *The Book of Jerry Falwell: Fundamentalist Language and Politics* (Princeton, NJ: Princeton: University Press, 2001); and Bruce Bawer, *Stealing Jesus: How Fundamentalism Betrays Christianity* (New York: Three Rivers Press, 1998).

22. See Michael Eric Dyson, *Between God and Gangsta Rap: Bearing Witness to Black Culture* (New York: Oxford University Press, 1996); Tex Sample, *White Soul: Country Music, the Church, and Working Americans* (Nashville: Abingdon Press, 1996); Dimitri Ehrlich, *Inside the Music: Conversations with Contemporary Musicians about Spirituality, Creativity, and Consciousness* (Boston: Shambala, 1997); and Juan Flores, *From Bomba to Hip-Hop: Puerto Rican Culture and Latino Identity* (New York: Columbia University Press, 2000).

23. See Peter J. Jankowski, "Postmodern Spirituality: Implications for Promoting Change," *Counseling and Values* (October 22, 2002): 69–79.

24. Ibid., 71.

25. James R. Brockman, SJ, ed., *The Violence of Love: The Pastoral Wisdom of Arch-bishop Oscar Romero* (San Francisco: Harper & Row, 1988), 54.
26. Dietrich Bonhoeffer, *Meditations on the Cross*, ed. Manfred Weber (Louisville, KY: Westminster John Knox Press, 1996), 87.
27. Marcus J. Borg, "From Galilean Jew to the Face of God: The Pre-Easter and Post-Easter Jesus," in *Jesus at 2000*, ed. Marcus J. Borg (Boulder, CO: West-view Press, 1998), 17.
28. See Megan McKenna, *Not Counting Women and Children* (Maryknoll, NY: Orbis Books, 1994), chap. 1.
29. Ibid., 17.
30. See Alister E. McGrath, *The Future of Christianity* (London: Blackwell , 2002); John Shelby Spong, *Why Christianity Must Change or Die: A Bishop Speaks to Believers in Exile* (San Francisco: HarperSanFrancisco, 1998); and Wade Clark Roof, et al., *The Post-War Generation and Establishment Religion* (Boulder, CO: Westview Press, 1995).

Chapter 4: The Good News Politics of Jesus

1. See Samuel P. Huntington, *The Clash of Civilizations and the Remaking of World Order* (New York: Touchstone, 1997). See also Daniel Philpott, "The Challenge of September 11 to Secularism in International Relations," *World Politics* 55, no. 1 (2002): 66–95. The current clash of civilizations between Islam and the West reflects two worldviews confronting each other, with each one claiming to have the true revelation of God. There has never been a shortage of individuals willing to give up their lives and that of innocent others to carry out the so-called will of God. Take, for example, the biblical story of Samson (Judg. 16:26–31), which can be read as equivalent to Atta's attack on the World Trade Center. See Shadia Drury, "Terrorism: From Samson to Atta," *Arab Studies Quarterly*, 25, nos. 1–2 (Winter/Spring 2003): 1–12.
2. Benjamin R. Barber, *Jihad vs. McWorld: Terrorism's Challenge to Democracy* (1995; repr., New York: Ballantine Books, 2001), xxiv.
3. See David Palumbo-Liu, "Multiculturalism Now: Civilization, National Identity, and Difference before and after September 11th," *Boundary* 2, no. 29 (Summer 2002): 127.
4. In his book *Democracy Matters: Winning the Fight against Imperialism* (New York: Penguin, 2004), Cornel West examines the arrested state of democratic culture in the United States with his brilliant brand of radical historicism and vision of democracy as a regulative ideal of life together. According to West, American democracy is captive to market fundamentalism, aggressive militarism, and escalating authoritarianism, which requires reawakening democratic vistas and the prophetic religious tradition. West thickens our vision by reminding us that democracy mattered to the black, white, and Jewish intellectuals and political leaders that shaped its cultural and institutional character. Yet carrying West's vision to the edges of a new imagining of how democracy matters means not only exploring more deeply what, for example, Dolores Huerta is doing with immigrant workers, but stating what Latinos contributed to shaping the American democratic tradition and what Latino immigration and transnational identity now suggests is part of the fundamental transformation and new imagining of democracy. For example, the work of Cesar E. Chavez, the cofounder of the United Farm Workers, contributed a great deal to the formation of the democratic tradition. For his labor rights, peace work,

and nonviolent activism Chavez was a recipient of the Martin Luther King Jr. Peace Prize during his lifetime, was awarded the Presidential Medal of Freedom by President Clinton on August 8, 1994, and received the Aquilia Aztec (the Aztec Eagle), Mexico's highest award presented to people of Mexican heritage who have made major contributions outside Mexico.

5. Robert N. Bellah, "The New American Empire: The Likely Consequence of the 'Bush Doctrine,'" in *Anxious about Empire: Theological Essays on the New Global Realities*, ed. Wes Avram (Grand Rapids: Brazos Press, 2004), 22.

6. George W. Bush, "Address to a Joint Session of Congress and the American People," White House Office of the Press Secretary, Washington, DC, September 20, 2001, http://www.whitehouse.gov/news/releases/2001/09/200109 20-8.html.

7. See Gilbert Achcar, *The Clash of Barbarisms: September 11 and the Making of the New World Disorder* (New York: Monthly Review Press, 2002); and Stanley Hauerwas and Frank Lentricchia, eds., *Dissent from the Homeland: Essays after September 11* (Durham, NC: Duke University Press, 2003).

8. Jürgen Moltmann, "Political Theology and Theology of Liberation," in *Liberating the Future: God, Mammon, and Theology*, ed. Joerg Rieger (Minneapolis: Fortress Press, 1998), 70. See also Mary Potter Engel, "Evil, Sin, and the Violation of the Vulnerable," in *Lift Every Voice: Constructing Christian Theologies from the Underside*, 2nd ed., ed. Susan Brooks Thistlethwaite and Mary Potter Engel (Maryknoll, NY: Orbis Books, 1998), 155.

9. Interestingly, President Bush's religio-political rhetoric evidenced in speeches describing his war on terrorism, like that of Osama bin Laden, is dualistic, absolutistic, and polarizing. Perhaps that is why some argue today that the conflict between Islam and the West originates in their similarities rather than their differences.

10. If Freud once questioned Woodrow Wilson's belief that God called him to the executive office, the faith-based presidency of George W. Bush, the man who consulted a "heavenly father" before sending troops into Iraq as an instrument of God's will and to establish freedom, should make us concerned about his sense of calling.

11. Audrey Chapman believes mainline churches are so accommodated to the socioeconomic life in America that they cannot seriously serve as transforming agents of the dominant order. Indeed, many in the church see it mostly as a volunteer association expressing little commitment to a God of justice, peace, and compassionate action. See Chapman, *Faith, Power and Politics: Political Ministry in Mainline Churches* (New York: Pilgrim Press, 1991).

12. See Kathryn Tanner, *The Politics of God* (Minneapolis: Fortress Press, 1992); Jürgen Moltmann, *The Crucified God* (New York: Harper & Row, 1974); and Gustavo Gutierrez, *The God of Life* (Maryknoll, NY: Orbis Books, 1991).

13. Mainline Christian denominations have tended to cluster around the center in their political engagement and vision of the common good, although movements for a more radical Christianity have surfaced in the course of American church history. For scholarship on the politically centrist tendency of mainline Christianity, see Robert Wuthnow and John H. Evans, eds., *The Quiet Hand of God* (Berkeley: University of California Press, 2002). For essays dealing with radical Christianity, see Michael L. Budde and Robert W. Brimlow, eds., *The Church as Counterculture* (Albany: State University of New York Press, 2000).

14. Jim Wallis, *The Soul of Politics* (New York: New Press; Maryknoll, NY: Orbis Books, 1994), 13–15.

15. See Wes Avram, ed., *Anxious about Empire*, 111.
16. See the chapter entitled "Ways toward the Political Liberation of Mankind," in Moltmann, *Crucified God*, 317–40.
17. National organizations promoting social justice and upholding democratic traditions include the Industrial Areas Foundation, the Gamaliel Foundation, Direct Access Resource Training, and the Pacific Institute for Community Organizing.
18. In *Faith in Action: Religion, Race, and Democratic Organizing in America* (Chicago: University of Chicago Press, 2002), Richard L. Wood argues that faith-based initiatives in grassroots communities both reform and critique public policy and contribute to building the political capacity of the most marginalized and disadvantaged communities. I find that a great insight of Wood's work is that the language of religion offers a conceptual framework for political activism rooted in a sense of common identity for persons of different ethnic and cultural backgrounds. Although the work recognizes that the interest of social change can be advanced or arrested by faith initiatives, Wood makes plain that faith communities can be instrumental in renewing democratic culture.
19. See Lester Kurtz and Kelly Goran Fulton, "Love Your Enemies? Protestants and United States Foreign Policy," in *The Quiet Hand of God: Faith-Based Activism and the Public Role of Mainline Protestantism*, ed. Robert Wuthnow and John H. Evans (Berkeley: University of California Press, 2002), 364–80; and Jack Nelson-Pallmeyer, *The Politics of Compassion* (Maryknoll, NY: Orbis Books, 1986).
20. See Steve Bruce, *Politics and Religion* (Cambridge, UK: Polity, 2003); and Mark R. Warren, *Dry Bones Rattling: Community Building to Revitalize American Democracy* (Princeton, NJ: Princeton University Press, 2001), which discusses how religious organizations build the social capital that especially restores devastated communities, serve as centers of learning and leadership, and build the community strength that revitalizes democratic institutions and traditions.
21. See Peter L. Berger, ed., *The Desecularization of Religion* (Grand Rapids: Wm. B. Eerdmans Publishing Co., 1999).
22. The social sciences expressed a keen interest in religion with the rise of political Christianity (conservative and liberationist) in the 1970s, fundamentalist Islamic movements in the Middle East, and social movements in Latin America, the United States, and Israel. See José Casanova, *Public Religions in the Modern World* (Chicago: University of Chicago Press, 1994); Martin Marty and Scott Appelby, *Fundamentalism Observed* (Chicago: University of Chicago Press, 1991); Christian Smith, *Disruptive Religion: The Force of Faith in Social Movement Activism* (New York: Routledge, 1996); and Peter Beyer, *Religion and Globalization* (London: Sage, 1994).
23. George Weigel, "Religion and Peace: An Argument Complexified," *Washington Quarterly* 14 (Spring 1991): 27.
24. John Ashcroft, then a senator from Missouri, best exemplified the new civil religious nationalism in a speech delivered at Bob Jones University on May 8, 1999, in which he suggested America "has no king but Jesus." Prior to becoming attorney general, his brand of religious nationalism made him the Christian Right's favorite politician.
25. Marci A. Hamilton, "Religion and the Law in the Clinton Era: An Anti-Madisonian Legacy," in *Law and Contemporary Problems* 63 (Winter-Spring 2000): 359.

26. Ibid., 337.
27. For ways religious beliefs influence political behavior, see David C. Leege and Lyman A. Kellstedt, *Rediscovering the Religious Factor in American Politics* (Armonk, NY: M. E. Sharpe, 1993); Aldon D. Morris, *The Origins of the Civil Rights Movement* (New York: Free Press, 1984); and Stephen Carter, *The Culture of Disbelief* (New York: Basic Books, 1993).
28. See "Religion on the Stump: Politics and Faith in America" in *A Pew Forum on Religion and Public Life Discussion*, http://www.pewforum.org/publications/reports/stump.pdf.
29. As quoted in David Chidester, *Patterns of Power: Religion and Politics in American Culture* (Englewood Cliffs, NJ: Prentice Hall, 1988), 196.
30. Gloria Borger, *U.S. News and World Report*, June, 14, 2004.
31. The will of God revealed by the crucified Christ does not easily lend itself to the White House's theology of domination, although Bush would have it his way.
32. See Bruce Lincoln, *Holy Terrors: Thinking about Religion after September 11* (Chicago: University of Chicago Press, 2003), 104–7.
33. That we possess the greatest nuclear arsenal in the world and operate on the basis of a so-called preventive war policy should suggest the need for a critical reflection on the cost of this discipleship. Data is available at http://truthandpolitics .org/military-US-world.php.
34. See Chidester, *Patterns of Power*.
35. The New Testament at no point projects God through militaristic imagery; rather, a compassionate posture is advocated by the idea of loving your enemies by feeding them, quenching their thirst, and by the logic of overcoming evil with good. This was the posture taken by Mahatma Gandhi, Martin Luther King Jr., Oscar Romero, and Cesar Chavez.
36. Phillip Goodchild, *Capitalism and Religion: The Price of Piety* (London: Routledge, 2002), 44.
37. President George W. Bush is today considered one of the most openly "religious presidents in generations," a fact examined in a documentary aired by PBS and written by Raney Aronson entitled "The Jesus Factor." The documentary examines both Bush's conversion experience and the effect of right-wing evangelical Christianity in politics.
38. Gilbert Achcar, *The Clash of Barbarians: September 11 and the Making of the New World Disorder* (New York: Monthly Review Press, 2002), 103.
39. Civil religion is understood here as an ordered system of meaning by which Americans live, act, and view aspects of civil life and human rights as sacred.
40. Richard E. Wentz, *The Culture of Religious Pluralism* (Boulder, CO: Westview Press, 1998), 53.
41. See Robert Bellah, "Civil Religion in America," *Daedalus* 96 (1967): 1–21.
42. As Robert Wuthnow argues, civil religion can in this regard be an arena of conflict between liberal and conservative Christian visions of society. See his "Divided We Fall: America's Two Civil Religions," *Christian Century*, April 20, 1988, 395–99.
43. Daisy L. Machado, "La Otra America—The Other America," in *A Dream Unfinished: Theological Reflection on America from the Margins*, ed. Eleazar S. Fernandez and Fernando Segovia, (Maryknoll, NY: Orbis Books, 2001), 225.
44. Mark Hatfield, "The Sin That Scarred Our National Soul," *Christian Century*, February 21, 1973, 221.

45. Moltmann, *Crucified God*, 324.
46. Edward Said, *Culture and Imperialism* (New York: Vintage, 1993), 300–301.
47. See Max L. Stackhouse, "Torture, Terrorism, and Theology: The Need for a Universal Ethic," *Christian Century*, October 8, 1986, 861–63; and Alister E. McGrath, *The Future of Christianity* (Malden, MA: Blackwell, 2002).
48. Stackhouse, "Torture, Terrorism, and Theology," 861.
49. Miroslav Volf, *Exclusion and Embrace: A Theological Exploration of Identity, Otherness, and Reconciliation* (Nashville: Abingdon Press, 1996), 24.
50. David Machacek argues that in the context of America's new religious pluralism, attributable to an increase in diversity by way of immigration, a new civil religious tradition is emerging that affirms religious diversity as a positive value. I suspect his hopeful view is more wishful thinking, however, especially that neoconservatives like Peter Brimelow and Samuel Huntington are alarmed that the new immigration threatens Anglo-Saxon Protestant culture; indeed, they are not even willing to embrace their Latino Christian brethren without.
51. Thomas Poole, "Black Religion and Civil Religion: African-American Voices in America's 'Third Time of Trial,'" *Journal of Theology for Southern Africa* 77, no. 1 (2001): 30.
52. On how the civil rights movement and Martin Luther King Jr. challenged white supremacist theology, see Mark Taylor, *The Executed God* (Minneapolis: Fortress Press, 2001).
53. Civil religion has been a topic of conversation for at least four decades in American society relative to the various ways it helps transfer allegiance to the larger structures of formally organized power in society, or how it challenges the institutionalized ways of government. Although civil religion promotes social integration in a pluralistic society, it has been criticized for excluding the public voice of women and expressing the views of white society by way of imagined narratives that ignore the historical experience of enslaved Africans, slaughtered Native Americans, and conquered Mexicans and Puerto Ricans.
54. West, *Democracy Matters*, 22.
55. For a historically important work on Latin American political Christologies, see José Miguez Bonino, ed., *Faces of Jesus: Latin American Christologies* (Maryknoll, NY: Orbis Books, 1977).
56. See Marcus J. Borg, *Conflict, Holiness, and Politics in the Teachings of Jesus*, 2nd ed. (Harrisburg, PA: Trinity Press International, 1988).
57. Ibid., 22–34.
58. See Michael Lerner, *The Politics of Meaning* (Cambridge, MA: Perseus Books, 1996).
59. On this perspective see John W. De Gruchy, "Christian Witness and the Transformation of Culture in a Society in Transition," in *Christ and Context*, ed. Hilary Regand and Alan J. Torrance (Edinburgh: T. &T. Clark, 1993), 131–52.
60. John Dominic Crossan, "Jesus and the Kingdom: Itinerants and Householders in Earliest Christianity," in *Jesus at 2000*, ed. Marcus J. Borg (Boulder, CO: Westview Press, 1998), 33.
61. Jürgen Moltmann, *God for a Secular Society* (Minneapolis: Fortress Press, 1999), 21.
62. See John Howard Yoder, *The Politics of Jesus* (Grand Rapids: Wm. B. Eerdmans Publishing Co., 1972).
63. See Jürgen Moltmann, *The Way of Jesus Christ* (Minneapolis: Fortress Press, 1993).

64. Ibid., 118.
65. See Marcus J. Borg, *Meeting Jesus again for the First Time* (New York: Harper-Collins, 1994), chap. 3.
66. Ibid., 52.
67. For a study that examines the religio-ethical paradigm shift initiated by Jesus from the ethic of holiness to that of compassion, see Borg, *Conflict, Holiness, and Politics in the Teachings of Jesus*.
68. Ibid., 53.
69. See Borg, *Conflict, Holiness, and Politics in the Teachings of Jesus*, 243–46.
70. Jon Sobrino, *The True Church and the Poor* (Maryknoll, NY: Orbis Books, 1984), 236.
71. Ibid., 295.
72. See Albert Nolan, *Jesus before Christianity*, 25th anniversary ed. (Maryknoll, NY: Orbis Books, 2001), chap. 13.
73. For an important essay on how mercy structured the ministry of Jesus, see Jon Sobrino, *The Principle of Mercy* (Maryknoll, NY: Orbis Books, 1994), chap. 1.
74. See Richard Cassidy, *Jesus, Politics, and Society: A Study of the Gospel of Luke* (Maryknoll, NY: Orbis Books, 1978).
75. For the most part, Latinos do not neatly compartmentalize their understanding of the sacred and the secular, which suggests that their influence in both U.S. society and its religious institutions will present "political Christianity" in various ways as reflected in the internal understandings and interpretations Latinos make that link individual faith and larger institutions. In her doctoral dissertation, Catherine Evans Wilson studied the three largest Latino faith-based organizations in the country. Her work suggests both the importance of understanding the political Christianity of the Latino community and the nature and contribution of Latino faith-based organizations to the renewal of U.S. political structures. See Wilson, "A Different Kind of Mandate: Latino Faith-Based Organizations and the Communitarian Impulse" (PhD diss., University of Pennsylvania, 2003).
76. On this theme in the context of Africa, see Adrea Makoye Ng'weshema, "Rediscovering the Human: Human Existence and the Quest for a Christo-theological Anthropology in Africa" (PhD diss., Lutheran School of Theology, Chicago, 1999).
77. Jack Nelson-Pallmeyer, *The Politics of Compassion* (Maryknoll, NY: Orbis Books, 1988), 115.

Chapter 5: The Church in a World Apart

1. M. Chaves, "National Congregations Study: Background, Methods, and Selected Results," *Journal for the Scientific Study of Religion* 38, no. 4 (Dec. 1999): 458–77. See also Michael Emerson and Karen Chai Kim, "Multiracial Congregations: An Analysis of Their Development and a Typology," *Journal for the Scientific Study of Religion* 42, no. 2 (June 2003): 217–28.
2. Because one of the principles of Americanism is embracing diverse points of view, the influence of Hispanic/Latino culture on American society will both inspire awareness of the deep sixteenth-century roots of Latinos in North America, the Indian ancestors of Chicanos, and the fact that Pancho Villa is not the villain Hollywood movies project, and will awaken interest in exploring the Hispanic frame of mind by reading Latino writers such as William Carlos Williams, Oscar Hijuelos, Rudolfo Anaya, Pedro Pietri, and Julia Alvarez (all of whom write in English).

3. The Christianity that is practiced by non-European immigrants in the United States, for instance, often demonstrates cultural differences from that of the mostly mainline denominational bodies with which they enter into membership. Indeed, the empirical evidence shows that post-1965 immigrants, unlike earlier groups, have not so much assimilated into the dominant religious culture as they have "de-Europeanized" it. See R. S. Warner, "Approaching Religious Diversity: Barriers, Byways, and Beginnings," *Sociology of Religion* 59 (1998): 193–215.

4. Church growth evangelists Donald McGavran and Peter Wagner affirm that God accepts culture, but their gospel marketing vision calls for congregations to grow by way of attracting the same kind of people—the homogenous principle. On the question of culture, McGavran tends to absolutize conventional culture and leave aside how the gospel questions negative elements within it (see Lesslie Newbigin, *The Gospel in a Pluralist Society* [Grand Rapids: Wm. B. Eerdmans Publishing Co., 1989]).

5. On communicating the gospel in diverse contexts see R. Daniel Shaw and Charles E. van Engen, *Communicating God's Word in a Complex World: God's Truth or Hocus Pocus?* (Lanham, MD: Rowman & Littlefield Publishers, 2003).

6. Ibid., 95.

7. David M. Rhoads, *The Challenge of Diversity: The Witness of Paul and the Gospels* (Minneapolis: Fortress Press, 1996), 1.

8. Albert C. Outler, *Evangelism and Theology in the Wesleyan Spirit* (Nashville: Discipleship Resources, 2000), 68.

9. Ibid., 2.

10. Ronald J. Sider, *Good News and Good Works* (Grand Rapids: Baker Books, 1993), 176.

11. In *Women, Religion, and Social Change in Brazil's Popular Church* (Notre Dame, IN: University of Notre Dame Press, 1997), Carol Ann Drogus discusses how the women who make up the majority of the membership in base Christian communities take the message of liberation theology, which is largely the product of male clerics, and live it from the standpoint of their own experience. In other words, gender differences are not only important for understanding the meaning of religion, but the social, cultural, and political change envisioned by liberation theology is given a distinctive identity by women who receive and interpret its message. Drogus's work suggests the importance of understanding the positive value of difference in religious communities not simply across cultural groups but within them as well.

12. After September 11, 2001, religion was not necessarily seen as a force for good that promotes peace in the world. In the interest of an evangelistic approach that fosters conversation across religious traditions and that promotes peace, I suggest that congregations study Harold Coward and Gordon S. Smith, eds., *Religion and Peacebuilding* (Albany: State University of New York Press, 2004).

13. George E. Tinker, *Spirit and Resistance: Political Theology and American Indian Liberation* (Minneapolis: Fortress Press, 2004), 114.

14. Jürgen Moltmann, *The Spirit of Life* (Minneapolis: Fortress Press, 1992), 115.

15. Eleanor W. Lynch and Marci J. Hanson, *Developing Cross-Cultural Competence* (Baltimore: Paul H. Brookes Publishing Co., 1993), 50.

16. See R. Stephen Warner and Judith G. Wittner, eds., *Gatherings in Diaspora: Religious Communities and the New Immigration* (Philadelphia: Temple University Press, 1998); and Helen Rose Ebaugh and Janet Saltzman Chafetz, *Religion and the New Immigrants: Continuities and Adaptations in Immigrant Congregations* (Walnut Creek, CA: AltaMira, 2000).

17. See Stephen A. Rhodes, *Where the Nations Meet: The Church in a Multicultural World* (Downers Grove, IL: InterVarsity Press, 1998).

18. Clifford Geertz, *The Interpretation of Cultures* (New York: Basic Books, 1973), 89.

19. James P. Spradley and David W. McCurdy, *Anthropology: The Cultural Perspective*, 2nd ed. (New York: Wiley, 1980), 1–2.

20. Margaret D. LeCompte and Jean J. Schensul, *Designing and Conducting Ethnographic Research* (Walnut Creek, CA: AltaMira Press, 1999), 24.

21. Charles R. Taber, *The World Is Too Much with Us* (Macon, GA: Mercer Press, 1991), 3–4.

22. See Wendy Griswold, *Cultures and Societies in a Changing World* (Thousand Oaks, CA: Pine Forge Press, 1994).

23. Brenda E. Brasher, *Give Me That Online Religion* (San Francisco: Jossey-Bass, 2001), 6.

24. I draw on the work of Spradley and McCurdy, *Anthropology*, chap. 1.

25. Ralph Linton, *The Study of Man: An Introduction* (New York: D. Appleton-Century Co., 1936), 326–27. Linton argues that only about 10 percent of one's cultural identity is not borrowed from other cultures.

26. Marcus J. Borg, *Conflict, Holiness, and Politics in the Teaching of Jesus* (Harrisburg, PA: Trinity Press International, 1984), 246.

27. Rhoads, *Challenge of Diversity*, 15.

28. Ibid.

29. Gerhard Lohfind, *Jesus and Community* (Minneapolis: Fortress Press, 1982), 88–89.

30. For a discussion of Jesus' linking the love of God and neighbor that is not limited by cultural rules and religious tradition, see Mary Ann Talbert, "Is It Lawful on the Sabbath to Do Good or to Do Harm? Mark's Ethic of Religious Practice," *Perspectives in Religious Studies* 23, no. 2 (2001): 199–214.

31. For ways that Jesus is an active transmitter of holiness and a rejecter of the cultural rules of contamination, see Borg, *Conflict, Holiness, and Politics in the Teaching of Jesus*.

32. See James E. Lamkin, "Location, Location, Location: A Homiletic Exegesis of John 4," *Review and Expositor* 96 (1999): 583–88.

33. Many persons within the dominant American culture learn to see women of color as ethnically inferior, morally questionable, and living in domestic "sin." Hence, these women share something with the Samaritan woman by the well of Jacob, and they come to Jesus expecting to be compassionately embraced.

34. For a helpful exegesis of this text in light of a multicultural reading see Judith Gundry-Volf, "Spirit, Mercy, and the Other," *Theology Today* 51, no. 4 (1995): 508–23.

35. Bernard J. F. Lonergan, *Method in Theology* (New York: Herder & Herder, 1972). See this work for a discussion for finding community through our differences.

36. Gundry-Volf, "Spirit, Mercy, and the Other," 513.

37. See Rhodes, *Where the Nations Meet*, chap. 7.

38. For a groundbreaking study of the racialized discourse of modern intellectual movements and their influence on biblical scholarship, see Shawn Kelley, *Racializing Jesus: Race, Ideology, and the Formation of Modern Biblical Scholarship* (London: Routledge, 2002).

Selected Reading

Religion and Society

Becker, P. E., and N. L. Eiesland, eds. *Contemporary American Religion: An Ethnographic Reader*. Walnut Creek, CA: AltaMira Press, 1997.

Ciminio, Richard, and Don Tattin. *Shopping for Faith: American Religion in the New Millenium*. San Francisco: Jossey-Bass, 1998.

Harding, Susan F. *The Book of Jerry Falwell: Fundamentalist Language and Politics*. Princeton, NJ: Princeton University Press, 2000.

Harris, F. *Loose Connections: Joining Together in America's Fragmented Communities*. Cambridge, MA: Harvard University Press, 1998.

———. *Something Within: Religion in African-American Political Activism*. New York: Oxford University Press, 1999.

Jenkins, Phillip. *The Next Christendom: The Coming of Global Christianity*. New York: Oxford University Press, 2002.

Lincoln, Bruce. *Holy Terrors: Thinking about Religion after September 11*. Chicago: University of Chicago Press, 2003.

Prentiss, Craig, ed. *Religion and the Creation of Race and Ethnicity*. New York: New York University Press, 2003.

Rieger, Joerg. *God and the Excluded: Visions and Blind Spots in Contemporary Theology*. Minneapolis: Fortress Press, 2001.

Roof, Wade Clark. *Spiritual Marketplace: Baby Boomers and the Remaking of American Religion*. Princeton, NJ: Princeton University Press, 1999.

Smith, C. S. *Disruptive Religion: The Force of Faith in Social Movement Activism*. New York: Routledge, 1996.

Stevens-Arroyo, Anthony M., and Gilbert R. Cadena, eds. *Old Masks, New Faces: Religion and Latino Identities*. New York: New York University Press, 1995.

Vasquez, Manuel A., and Marie Friedmann Marguardt. *Globalizing the Sacred: Religion across the Americas*. New Brunswick, NJ: Rutgers University Press, 2003.

Wuthnow, Robert. *After Heaven: Spirituality in America since the 1950s*. Berkeley: University of California Press, 1998.

Latino/a Theology and Church

Banuelas, Arturo, ed. *Mestizo Christianity: Theology from the Latino Perspective*. Maryknoll, NY: Orbis Books, 1995.

De la Torre, Miguel, and Edwin David Aponte. *Introducing Latino/a Theologies*. Maryknoll, NY: Orbis Books, 2001.

Elizondo, Virgilio. *Galilean Journey: The Mexican-American Promise*. Maryknoll, NY: Orbis Books, 1983.

Fernandez, Eduardo. *La Cosecha: Harvesting Contemporary United States Hispanic Theology (1972–1998)*. Collegeville, MN: Liturgical Press, 2001.

Goizueta, Roberto S., ed. *We Are a People! Initiatives in Hispanic American Theology*. Minneapolis: Fortress Press, 1992.

González, Justo. *Mañana: Christian Theology from a Hispanic Perspective*. Nashville: Abingdon Press, 1990.

Isasi-Diaz, Ada Maria. *En La Lucha/in the Struggle: Elaborating a Mujerista Theology*. Minneapolis: Fortress Press, 2003.

Machado, Daisy L., María Pilar Aquino, and Jeanette Rodríguez, eds. *A Reader in Latina Feminist Theology: Religion and Justice*. Austin: University of Texas Press, 2002.

Maldonardo, David, ed. *Protestantes/Protestants: Hispanic Christianity within Mainline Tradition*. Nashville: Abingdon Press, 1999.

Pedraja, Luis G. *Teologia: An Introduction to Hispanic Theology*. Nashville: Abingdon Press, 2004.

Asian Theology and Church

Bock, Kim Young, ed. *Minjung Theology: People as the Subjects of History*. Singapore: Commission on Theological Concerns, 1981.

Fabella, Virginia, ed. *Asia's Struggle for Full Humanity*. Maryknoll, NY: Orbis Books, 1980.

Lee, Jung Young. *Marginality: The Key to Multicultural Theology*. Minneapolis: Fortress Press, 1995.

Matsuoka, Fumitaka. *Out of Silence: Emerging Themes in Asian American Churches*. Cleveland: United Church Press, 1995.

Park, Andrew Sung. *Racial Conflict and Healing: An Asian-American Theological Perspective*. Maryknoll, NY: Orbis Books, 1996.

Pui-Lan, Kwok. *Discovering the Bible in the Non-Biblical World*. Maryknoll, NY: Orbis Books, 1995.

———. *Introducing Asian Feminist Theology*. Sheffield, UK: Sheffield Academic Press, 2000.

Native American Theology

Deloria, Vine, ed. *For This Land: Writings on Religion in America*. New York: Routledge, 1999.

Tinker, George E. *Missionary Conquest: The Gospel and Native American Genocide*. Minneapolis: Fortress Press, 1995.

Tinker, George E., Clara Sue Kidwell, and Homer Noley. *A Native American Theology*. Maryknoll, NY: Orbis Books, 2003.

African American Theology and Church

Billingsley, A. *Mighty Like a River: The Black Church and Social Reform*. New York, Oxford University Press, 2000.

Cannon, Katie. *Black Womanist Theology*. Atlanta: American Academy of Religion, 1988.

Cone, James. *Risks of Faith: The Emergence of a Black Theology of Liberation, 1968–1998*. Boston: Beacon Press, 1999.

Douglas, Kelly Brown. *Sexuality and the Black Churches: A Womanist Perspective*. Maryknoll, NY: Orbis Books, 1999.

Kelly, Shawn. *Racializing Jesus: Race, Ideology and the Formation of Modern Biblical Scholarship*. New York: Routledge, 2002.

Lincoln, C. Eric, and Lawrence H. Mamiya. *The Black Church in the African-American Experience*. Durham, NC: Duke University Press, 1990.

Pinn, Anthony. *The Black Church in the Post-Civil Rights Era*. Maryknoll, NY: Orbis Books, 2002.

Pinn, Anthony B., and Benjamin Valentin, eds. *Ties That Bind: African American and Hispanic American/Latino Theologies in Dialogue*. New York: Continuum, 2001.

Williams, Delores. *Sisters in the Wilderness*. Maryknoll, NY: Orbis Books, 1993.

Wimbush, Vincent. *African Americans and the Bible*. New York: Continuum, 2000.

Practical Theology and Culture

Ammerman, Nancy T., Jackson W. Carroll, Carl S. Dudley, and William McKinney, eds. *Studying Congregations: A New Handbook*. Nashville: Abingdon Press, 1998.

Angrosino, Michael V. *Talking about Cultural Diversity in Your Church*. Walnut Creek, CA: Altamira Press, 2001.

Foster, Charles R., and Theodore Brelsford. *We Are the Church Together: Cultural Diversity in Congregational Life*. Valley Forge, PA: Trinity Press International, 1996.

Hopewell, James F. *Congregation: Stories and Structures*. Philadelphia: Fortress Press, 1987.

McGuire, Meredith B. *Religion, the Social Context*. 5th ed. Belmont, CA: Wadsworth Thomson Learning, 2002.

Schensul, Jean J., and Margaret D. LeCompte, eds. *Ethnographer's Toolkit*. Walnut Creek, CA: AltaMira Press, 1999.

Tanner, Kathryn. *Theories of Culture: A New Agenda for Theology*. Minneapolis: Fortress Press, 1997.

Volf, Miroslav, and Dorothy C. Bass. *Practicing Theology: Beliefs and Practices in Christian Life*. Grand Rapids: Wm. B. Eerdmans Publishing Co., 2002.

Warner, R. Stephen. *New Wine in Old Wineskins*. Berkeley: University of California Press, 1988.

Webb, Joseph M. *Preaching and the Challenge of Pluralism*. St. Louis: Chalice Press, 1998.

Multiracial Relations

Alex-Assensoh, Yvette M., and Lawrence J. Hanks, eds. *Black and Multiracial Politics in America*. New York: New York University Press, 2000.

Davis, Mike. *Magical Urbanism: Latinos Reinvent the U.S. City*. London: Verso, 2000.

Marable, Manning. *Beyond Black and White: Transforming African-American Politics*. London: Verso, 1995.

Piatt, Bill. *Black and Brown in America: The Case for Cooperation*. New York: New York University Press, 1997.

Vaca, Nicolas. *The Presumed Alliance: The Unspoken Conflict between Latinos and Blacks and What It Means for America*. New York: HarperCollins, 2004.

Wilson, William Julius. *The Bridge over the Racial Divide: Rising Inequality and Coalition Politics*. Berkeley: University of California Press, 1999.

Religion and Gender

Castelli, Elizabeth, ed. *Women, Gender, and Religion: A Reader*. New York: Palgrave, 2001.

Eilberg-Schwartz, Howard, and Wendy Doniger, eds. *Off with Her Head! The Denial of Women's Identity in Myth, Religion, and Culture*. Berkeley: University of California, 1995.

Scripture Index

Subject Index